Teaching
Sports Media

AF234697

Master Class
Resources for Teaching Mass Communication
Series Editor: Chris Roberts (University of Alabama)

Master Class: Teaching Advice for Journalism and Mass Communication Instructors, by the AEJMC Elected Standing Committee on Teaching, edited by Chris Roush. 2017.

Testing Tolerance: Addressing Controversy in the Journalism and Mass Communication Classroom, by the AEJMC Commission on the Status of Women, edited by Candi Carter Olson and Tracy Everbach. 2020.

The Graduate Student Guidebook: From Orientation to Tenure Track, by the AEJMC Board of Directors, edited by Katherine A. Foss. 2020.

Teaching Race: Struggles, Strategies, and Scholarship for the Mass Communication Classroom, by The AEJMC Minorities and Communication Division, edited by George L. Daniels and Robin Blom. 2021.

Teaching Media Ethics: Integrating Ethics Across the Mass Communication Curriculum, by The AEJMC Media Ethics Division, edited by Nicole Kraft and Kathleen Bartzen Culver. 2024.

Instructing Intersectionality: Critical and Practical Application in the Journalism and Mass Communication Classroom, by The AEJMC Lesbian, Gay, Bisexual, Transgender & Queer Interest Group, edited by Nathian Shae Rodriguez. 2025.

Teaching Sports Media: Classroom Strategies for Getting Your Students in the Game, by The AEJMC Sports Communication Interest Group, edited by Welch Suggs and Lauren Smith. 2026.

About AEJMC

The Association for Education in Journalism and Mass Communication (AEJMC) is a nonprofit organization of more than 3,700 educators, students, and practitioners from around the globe. Founded in 1912 by Willard Grosvenor Bleyer, the first president (1912–1913) of the American Association of Teachers of Journalism, as it was then known, AEJMC is the oldest and largest alliance of journalism and mass communication educators and administrators at the college level. AEJMC's mission is to promote the highest possible standards for journalism and mass communication education, to encourage the widest possible range of communication research, to encourage the implementation of a multicultural society in the classroom and curriculum, and to defend and maintain freedom of communication in an effort to achieve better professional practice, a better-informed public, and wider human understanding.

About the Series Editor

Chris Roberts is an associate professor in the College of Communication and Information Sciences at The University of Alabama, and head of its Office of Research in Media Integrity. He began his media career as a disk jockey, and teenage sportswriter for the weekly *Jacksonville News* and daily *Anniston Star* in Calhoun County, Ala. He was a reporter and editor at daily newspapers in the Southeast before earning his doctoral degree at the University of South Carolina. He is a longtime member of the Society of Professional Journalists' ethics committee and part of the team that revised SPJ's ethics code in 2014. Dr. Roberts is co-author of *Doing Ethics in Media: Theories and Practical Applications* (Routledge, 2021). With AEJMC, he served as head of the Council of Divisions, served two terms on its Elected Standing Committee on Teaching, and in 2024 received its Dorothy Bowles Award for Outstanding Public Service.

Teaching Sports Media

Classroom Strategies for Getting Your Students in the Game

The AEJMC Sports Communication Interest Group

EDITED BY

Welch Suggs
University of Georgia, USA

Lauren Reichart Smith
Rowan University, USA

BLOOMSBURY ACADEMIC
NEW YORK • LONDON • OXFORD • NEW DELHI • SYDNEY

BLOOMSBURY ACADEMIC
Bloomsbury Publishing Inc, 1359 Broadway, New York, NY 10018, USA
Bloomsbury Publishing Plc, 50 Bedford Square, London, WC1B 3DP, UK
Bloomsbury Publishing Ireland, 29 Earlsfort Terrace, Dublin 2, D02 AY28, Ireland

BLOOMSBURY, BLOOMSBURY ACADEMIC and the Diana logo are trademarks of Bloomsbury
Publishing Plc

Copyright © Bloomsbury Publishing, Inc 2026

Cover design: Chloe Batch
Cover image © iStock.com/supriadi supriadi, fonikum, Enis Aksoy

All rights reserved. No part of this publication may be: i) reproduced or transmitted in any form,
electronic or mechanical, including photocopying, recording or by means of any information storage or
retrieval system without prior permission in writing from the publishers; or ii) used or reproduced in
any way for the training, development or operation of artificial intelligence (AI) technologies, including
generative AI technologies. The rights holders expressly reserve this publication from the text and data
mining exception as per Article 4(3) of the Digital Single Market Directive (EU) 2019/790.

Bloomsbury Publishing Inc does not have any control over, or responsibility for, any third-party
websites referred to or in this book. All internet addresses given in this book were correct at the
time of going to press. The author and publisher regret any inconvenience caused if addresses have
changed or sites have ceased to exist, but can accept no responsibility for any such changes.

Library of Congress Cataloging-in-Publication Data
Names: Association for Education in Journalism author | Suggs, Welch editor |
Smith, Lauren Reichart, 1977–editor
Title: Teaching sports media : classroom strategies for getting your students
in the game / The AEJMC Sports Communication Interest Group;
edited by Welch Suggs, Lauren Reichart Smith.
Description: New York : Bloomsbury Academic, 2026. | Series: Master class: resources
for teaching mass communication | Includes bibliographical references and index.
Identifiers: LCCN 2025038588 (print) | LCCN 2025038589 (ebook) |
ISBN 9798216278023 hardback | ISBN 9798216278030 paperback |
ISBN 9798216278047 epub | ISBN 9798216278054 pdf
Subjects: LCSH: Sports journalism—Study and teaching | Sports journalism—Authorship |
Online journalism—Study and teaching
Classification: LCC PN4784.S6 A727 2026 (print) | LCC PN4784.S6 (ebook) |
DDC 070.4/49796—dc23/eng/20250922
LC record available at https://lccn.loc.gov/2025038588
LC ebook record available at https://lccn.loc.gov/2025038589

ISBN: HB: 979-8-216-27802-3
PB: 979-8-216-27803-0
eBook: 979-8-216-27804-7
ePDF: 979-8-216-27805-4

Series: Master Class: Resources for Teaching Mass Communication

Typeset by Newgen KnowledgeWorks Pvt. Ltd., Chennai, India
Printed and bound in the United States of America

For product safety related questions contact productsafety@bloomsbury.com

To find out more about our authors and books visit www.bloomsbury.com
and sign up for our newsletters.

Contents

Introduction

Welch Suggs, The University of Georgia, and Lauren Reichart Smith, Rowan University

In the 2010s and 2020s, sports media programs have multiplied on college campuses across the United States. Shoring up flagging enrollment in communications and journalism, the growth of sports media mirrors the earlier rise of sport management programs in the 1990s, which similarly capitalized on student interest in athletics. Sports media taps into a deep cultural passion, offering students a pathway to careers that feel both exciting and relevant. As journalism schools look for ways to remain viable, sports media has emerged as a strategic lifeline, drawing in students who might otherwise bypass media studies altogether.

Communications schools and colleges are adopting different approaches to sports media. Some offer full majors in sports journalism, sport communication and sports media, such as Rowan University, Temple University, and the University of Nebraska. Others sponsor minors, including the University of Alabama. The University of Georgia and others offer certificates outside of major fields. Some, such as Northwestern, have a concentration within journalism majors. And several, such as Saint Bonaventure University, offer graduate programs in sports media.

Hull et al. (2019) provide a foundational exploration of the emergence of sports communication programs in higher education. Using the student–customer model as a theoretical lens, they argue that the proliferation of these programs is largely driven by institutional needs to attract and retain students amid declining enrollments in traditional journalism. Their qualitative study of program coordinators reveals that student interest, administrative support, and existing faculty expertise are critical to launching and sustaining successful programs. However, they also highlight challenges such as limited resources, administrative ambivalence, and the perception of sports media as less academically rigorous.

Building on this foundation, Coche and Haught (2021) examine how sports media curricula are adapting to the digital age. Their mixed-methods survey of faculty at ACEJMC-accredited institutions reveals that while programs are increasingly incorporating social media and branding instruction, the focus remains heavily on self-branding and posting live on social media. The authors argue that this narrow approach may leave students underprepared for the broader demands of a media landscape that now includes strategic communication, multimedia storytelling, and platform-specific content creation. They call for a more expansive integration of digital tools and branding concepts, noting that the line between journalism and public relations is increasingly blurred in sports media careers.

Etheridge and Bien-Aimé (2025) extended the conversation by situating sports media education within a broader sociocultural and geopolitical context. They argued that while many programs emphasize professional preparation, there is a pressing need to incorporate critical perspectives rooted in the MediaSport framework. Their commentary highlights how sports media intersects with global politics, economics, and identity, citing examples such as sportswashing, athlete activism, and the rise of athlete-driven media platforms. They advocate for curricula that balance applied skills with critical inquiry, enabling students to understand and challenge the power structures embedded in sports media.

Taken together, these three articles illustrate a trajectory in sports media education from pragmatic program development (Hull et al., 2019), to curricular adaptation to digital trends (Coche & Haught, 2021), to a call for deeper theoretical and ethical engagement (Etheridge & Bien-Aimé, 2025). While all three acknowledge the vocational appeal of sports media programs, they differ in emphasis: Hull et al. focus on institutional strategy, Coche and Haught on pedagogical practice, and Etheridge and Bien-Aimé on disciplinary legitimacy and critical consciousness.

Some sports media initiatives have emerged from mass communication studies departments and others out of more practitioner-focused programs in journalism, public relations, and other fields. When considering how to shape sports media curricula, faculty need to consider their goals and how those goals fit into broader institutional goals. Do they want to focus on preparing students for graduate study in sports communication? Are they preparing students for industry? What academic and professional backgrounds will teaching faculty have? The answers to these questions will determine how any individual program should structure its courses.

The purpose of this book is to help faculty develop new classes and update existing ones in sports media. We focus primarily on practitioner-focused courses, along with two chapters discussing courses on the intersection of sports, media, and society.

Chapter Summaries

We begin the first three chapters with different pedagogical approaches. "Ethics and Professionalism," by Nicole Kraft of The Ohio State University explores the ethical dilemmas students are likely to face in sport journalism and provides different assignments and practical strategies to teach students how to think through the ethics of a situation. Brian Mortiz of St. Bonaventure University takes us online and talks through the strategies to develop not only courses online, but also how to create an entire program online. Finally, Tammy Rae Matthews of St. Bonaventure University discusses ways to make our courses more accessible to students with different physical abilities and neurodivergencies, as well as how to cover adaptive sports.

The next section includes five chapters that examine specific courses that prepare students for various fields and industries. Drawing from his experience as a sports broadcaster and years of teaching sports broadcasting students, Kevin Hull from the University of South Carolina provides an overview of how to teach sports broadcasting. Betsy Emmons of the University of Nebraska-Lincoln provides an overview of the skill development areas in sports public relations. She provides ideas for class topics as well as potential assignments that allow students to practically apply the skills they have learned. From Northwestern University, Candy Lee focuses on the area of sports marketing, walking us through the topics that can be covered in a sports marketing course, with examples of discussion points and class activities that can be incorporated. Cara Hawkins-Jedlicka of Washington State University leverages the rapidly changing landscape of college athletes and sponsorship opportunities (Name, Image, and Likeness deals) to teach students about branding and self-presentation. Esports is the newest area to sports communication and curriculums. Kacey Doran of Rowan University discusses what type of faculty to hire for an esports class or curriculum, as well as an overview of general curriculum ideas.

The book recognizes that experiential learning is vital for sports media students, and it devotes three chapters to helping instructors find and maintain partnerships with organizations that offer places for students to publish, intern, work, and learn. Welch Suggs of the University of Georgia offers some nuts-and-bolts insight into providing students access to coverage of high school, collegiate, and professional sports. Steve Fox, of the University of Massachusetts at Amherst, shares his experiences in partnering courses with local and national media organizations to provide journalism students with a hands-on, experiential learning experience. Nick Hirshon of William Paterson University walks us through using a course to revive a student newspaper, accessing private resources to mentor students and provide experiential-learning opportunities.

We continue with two chapters focused on teaching ideas in sports classes that are bigger than the games. Karen Turner and Claire Smith of Temple University discuss how to approach difficult conversations about race, gender, and other topics that are challenging in the best circumstances and fraught in the current climate. Also, Michael Mirer from the University of Wisconsin-Milwaukee rounds things out with a discussion of teaching about the intersection of sports and society as a capstone to get students to make critical links between what they see in sports and media theory.

For the final chapter, we have taken a 'teaching lab' approach and offer advice from our contributors on how to handle situations in the classroom, and/or suggest specific assignments or activities we have found useful.

Conclusion

We hope this book will serve as a valuable resource for faculty planning new courses or refreshing existing ones. As you navigate the evolving landscape of sports media education, we also encourage you to connect with the Sports Communication Interest Group of AEJMC, as well as the International Association for Communication and Sport (IACS) and the Sport Communication Interest Group of ICA. These groups offer programming on pedagogy and research at their annual conferences and regular updates during the academic year.

The future of sports media education lies in a hybrid model—one that equips students with industry-relevant skills while also fostering critical thinking about the cultural, political, and ethical dimensions of sports communication. As the field continues to grow, educators must navigate the tension between market-driven imperatives and the academic responsibility to cultivate informed, reflective media professionals.

References

Coche, R., & Haught, M. J. (2021). Sports media education's evolution: Integrating technology, branding and strategic media. *Teaching Journalism & Mass Communication*, *11*(2), 27–36. https://aejmc.us/spig/wp-content/uploads/sites/9/2021/12/TJMC-11.2-Coche-Haught.pdf

Etheridge, C. E., & Bien-Aimé, S. (2025). After 50 years of sports media scholarship, the academy takes notice. *Sport History Review*. https://doi.org/10.1123/shr.2024-0040

Hull, K., Choi, M., & Kian, E. M. (2019). Examining the growth of sports communication programs in higher education through a questionnaire of program coordinators. *Journalism & Mass Communication Educator*, *74*(4), 407–421. https://doi.org/10.1177/1077695819835044

Part I
Pedagogy

1 Ethics and Professionalism

Nicole Kraft, The Ohio State University

A student who joined me in covering a professional game stood up and clapped when the home team scored a goal, despite being instructed multiple times that there was no cheering in the press box. A member of our student radio club asked if he could use a media credential to attend a women's basketball game against a highly ranked opponent as a fan. These moments remind me: Teaching sports journalism ethics isn't just about rules—it's about helping students navigate when passion collides with responsibility.

We love sports because they are emotional, high-stakes and personal—the ultimate reality show. To cover them professionally, however, students must learn to set aside their passions to focus on standards of accuracy, fairness and independence. As instructors, we need to teach more than just what the ethical challenges are—we need to show students how to recognize and respond to them.

Many assume sports journalists don't uphold mainstream journalism standards, and they have plenty of examples to prove them right. Broadcasters where I am in Columbus, Ohio, wear Ohio State scarlet and grey on gameday broadcasts and end their news segments with a cry of "Go Bucks!" The city's ABC affiliate's social media team reacted to a 2025 Cotton Bowl play in which the Buckeyes beat the University of Texas-Austin with this post: "JACK SAWYER TO THE MOTHER F*CKING HOUSE WITH A SCOOP AND SCORE!!!!!!!!!!!!!!!!!" The digital age has only intensified the challenges we face, with pressure to break news first and engage fans with specific sites and accounts. This has put sports journalists in a precarious situation, needing to balance accuracy, privacy and editorial independence in an ever-more-competitive business.

This chapter will explore the core ethical dilemmas that arise in sports journalism—fandom, access, anonymity, social media, AI, and more—and provide practical, classroom-tested ways to teach students how to think ethically, act professionally and hold themselves accountable.

Teaching Ethical Vigilance Early

The sports journalism road is paved with opportunity, but also with temptations. Student reporters today have unprecedented access to online stats, interviews, press releases and game footage. That same access opens the door to ethical shortcuts: plagiarism, fabrication, laziness and overreliance on tools like open AI. It's not enough to warn students about dangers—we must give them the tools to recognize and resist them, and to understand why shortcuts damage their credibility and the reputation of journalism itself.

Let's begin with foundational ethical theories:

- Utilitarianism (What outcome helps the most people and damages the fewest?)
- Communitarianism (How can the needs of the community and the individual be balanced?)
- Deontology (What is the right thing to do, regardless of outcome?), which incorporates the Categorical Imperative (If you knew your actions would become universal law, what would you do?)
- Virtue Ethics (What would a good journalist do?)

You can learn more about foundational ethical theories in Patrick Plaisance's chapter "Media Ethics Defined" in Plaisance (2024), and encourage students to use them as they approach a variety of ethical scenarios. Let's start with the broadest perspective.

In-Class Discussion: "Would You Ever…?"

To get started teaching sports ethics, I open the semester with a frank conversation (you can use a clicker poll, online form or anonymous response system) asking "would you:"

- copy a quote from a press release?
- use quotes from the story of someone who did not attend the press conference?
- use open AI to summarize a game you didn't watch, if you double-check the facts?
- publish a team press release verbatim?
- make up a quote from a source?

We then discuss the results. The goal isn't to call anyone out for potentially unethical behavior, but rather to create a safe space to see where students are and draw clear ethical lines. This helps them see the need for original sourcing and the significance of reader trust in the content we produce.

Classroom Policy

One of the best aspects of teaching sports journalism is the opportunity to cover real sporting events and teams in real time, but we must concurrently enforce real ethics. Given the many ways sports journalists can compromise ethical standards—from forming close relationships with sources to becoming entangled in fandom—it's essential to provide students with a clear framework to guide decision-making. That's where professional codes of ethics come in.

Every semester, we start our sports journalism path with an ethical analysis, performing a side-by-side comparison of the Associated Press Sports Editors Ethics Recommendations (2025) and the Society of Professional Journalists Code of Ethics (2014). The APSE Code has been narrowed down to four content areas:

- Conflicts of Interest
- Anonymous Sources
- Social Media
- Artificial Intelligence (AI).

The SPJ Code similarly has four content areas, with sub-categories underneath each:

- Seek Truth and Report It
- Minimize Harm
- Act Independently
- Be Accountable and Transparent.

In small groups, I ask our class to explore the areas of each code and compare the advice provided. Where, if anywhere, do they conflict? Are they complementary? Are they specific enough? What is missing? Each group then presents a summary of what they find and offers one practical reporting policy for each one of the key areas.

Digging into the Code

The Associated Press Sports Editors has long been a guiding voice in the industry. In 2025, the organization released updated recommendations aimed at newsrooms and digital-first environments. Its themes offer perfect prompts for real-world analysis, decision-making and conversation.

Conflicts of Interest

A "conflict of interest" is defined as having a personal connection or relationship that could potentially influence their reporting, leading to biased coverage and compromising the integrity of their writing. In sports, this can take many forms, from building an overly friendly relationship with coaches and players, to cheering openly for a favorite team, to using insider access for special treatment like autographs.

With students covering their own college's sports, this presents a whole new set of challenges, considering they might be friends with players or, at a minimum, classmates and partners on projects. Those same players who face a journalist's microphone on Saturday afternoon may be at the same bar with a reporter on Saturday night, which brings up the ethical issue of privacy.

A more significant conflict faced by student journalists is the element of fandom that potentially permeates all coverage. How should a student sports reporter, who likely picked their college in part because of the sports teams, separate themselves from the cult of fandom and the desire to cheer a beloved team to victory? Pre-writing is a big part of game coverage, due to the speed of publication. I had a student sports editor in 2024 who could not bring himself to pre-write/research a story based on an Ohio State football loss to its biggest rival, the University of Michigan, so traumatic was it for him to consider the possibility of defeat. We argued about the need to do it–right up until it was clear the Buckeyes were indeed losing to the Wolverines for the fourth straight time.

It has been drilled into every sports writer that cheering in the press box is one of the cardinal sins of sports journalism, and it applies equally in the collegiate sports world. Wearing spirit wear, even school colors, is a conflict and considered inappropriate behavior for those who occupy coverage space. To be a student journalist means checking more than just fandom. It is checking self-identification at the door. There is no "us" or "we" even though their tuition dollars provide some feeling of ownership.

In-Class Activity: "Fan or Journalist?" Simulation

Working with our sports information directors, we get a student-athlete to take part in a mock press conference that we stipulate is being held after a big game loss (every athlete knows this feeling). We ask them to be emotionally vulnerable where reasonable. The class, acting as reporters, ask postgame questions.

Afterward, we reflect as a group with the SID and the athlete:

- What were the best and worst questions, and why?
- Did anyone hold back important questions? If so, why?
- Did anyone ask an inappropriate or overly aggressive question?
- How did the reporters feel asking questions?
- How were the questions perceived by the athlete?
- What could we do better to balance empathy and the need for the public to know?

We then use this as a springboard to reinforce the role of emotional distance in ethical reporting. Difficult interviews will happen, and we need to know how to handle them professionally.

Getting a Gift

The journalistic rules on receiving gifts are usually pretty simple—don't take them. Many publications have financial limits (nothing worth more than $25, for example). But we also need to acknowledge that sports coverage comes with perks—and challenges.

In-Class Debate: What Would You Take?

Here is a list of scenarios: Ask students to vote "Accept" or "Decline":

- A press box meal before a game
- A rally towel placed on every seat
- A $150 backpack handed out to credentialed media at a bowl game
- A ride on the team charter plane
- A player-signed jersey for a friend
- Credentialed entry to a game the student isn't covering

Then split the class into teams and assign each one a scenario to argue. Ask them to justify their position using:

- APSE or SPJ codes
- Precedent or policy at real outlets (bring in examples!)

We finish by creating a class list of "Acceptable Perks" and "Ethical Red Flags."

Anonymous Sources

In sports journalism, insider information is coveted, especially in the collegiate environment where most access and messaging is managed through sports information directors. Separating from the reporting pack with behind-the-scenes information may rely on unnamed sources, but such usage comes with caveats. The goal is to instill in students an understanding of when and why anonymous sources should be used, the ethical and legal implications, and the potential impact on journalistic credibility.

Activity: Anonymous Sources

We provide students with hypothetical sports stories that rely on anonymous sources (for example, a leaked story about academic pressure to pass a student-athlete, an unreported and questionable NIL deal or a team accused of hazing).

The class is divided into small groups, each charged with deciding whether or not to use an anonymous source, considering the following questions:

- Does the information seem credible?
- Are there potential conflicts of interest or biases?
- How would they verify the claims made by the anonymous source?
- What are the risks and benefits of reporting the story? After each group presents its conclusions, hold a class-wide debate on the ethical implications of using the anonymous source.
- Should journalists be more cautious about relying on anonymous sources, or is the public interest paramount?
- How do you balance the need for exclusivity and breaking a story with the duty to provide accurate and fair reporting?

Social Media

The rise in social media has provided access to publishing platforms and sources like never before. Have breaking news or an opinion about a game or player performance? Post it! Interested in a player's personal life? Follow them on Instagram. Want to keep up with a team's media relations news? Follow them on X. Curious how fans feel about the team? Follow hashtags related to teams or players.

The ethical challenges surrounding social media are just as complex and varied as the opportunities. The ability to publish quickly is breathtaking for sport reporters who seek to share news first, but our journalism friends must balance the speed and accessibility of social media with the ethical responsibilities of accurate reporting, transparency and professionalism.

Journalists must also consider their use of social media, as posting personal opinions can skew perceptions of impartiality. There is no such thing as private on social media, even if you think only friends and family can see your accounts. Everything you share can be shared by others, including personal attacks, biased statements or controversial conversations.

We get the conversation started with these prompts:

- When does something shared on social media become newsworthy?
- What are the ethical guidelines journalists should follow when interacting with athletes or teams on social media?
- What is the difference between personal opinions and professional responsibilities on social media?

Use the answers as a catalyst toward this activity:

Social Media Source Verification Exercise

1   I present students with a real or hypothetical sports story, such as a player tweeting about a potential injury or a third party revealing on Instagram that a coach made controversial statements about his players' work ethics. We use a fake X or Instagram post generator and I populate the messaging platform Slack with other posts from accounts that are both "real" and "fan-oriented."

2   The class is split into small groups to assess the credibility of the social media post by:

- Identifying the source of the information (Is it an official account? A verified athlete? A fan account?).
- Checking for any conflicting information from other reputable sources.
- Determining if the post has been corroborated by other media outlets.

3 Each group then shares their perspectives, focusing on how to ethically verify social media information, the potential consequences of reporting unverified content and how journalists can keep reporting objectively.

Artificial Intelligence

The day the Associated Press told me I need not cover a hockey game because it would use artificial intelligence for the gamer, I knew sports writing had been changed forever. The ability to put in a box score and generate a story is a concerning aspect of OpenAI. But it also offers powerful tools for data analysis. Ever use Otter.ai to transcribe an interview? That's AI. Ever use Grammarly to improve writing? That's AI, too. AI can be used ethically to help with writing, question development, sourcing, stat analysis and more. The goal is to help students understand those benefits while avoiding some of the bigger pitfalls that can come from it, like using Open AI for story creation.

To begin developing an ethical understanding of OpenAI engagement, explain common tools and how they are used. I begin with a class demonstration using Copilot, ChatGPT or other AI to analyze a game article I have written—both the draft form and the final product. I ask specific questions about how the article can be improved, what material might be missing, and any spelling or grammar issues. Next, we ask it to revise the article and compare the OpenAI version to my version. Finally, I give it a box score from the game and ask it to write a gamer, and then we compare how that is similar or different, more or less engaging than the original or revised version.

We do a similar activity with a press release.

We also show what a transcription looks like using Otter.ai, both with a microphone close up and from a distance to evaluate quality. We also use audio from an athlete who is not a native English speaker, so they can see how accuracy can change. To help students understand the need for maintaining journalistic ethics when incorporating OpenAI into their reporting processes, we engage them with questions like:

- What are the benefits of using OpenAI in sports journalism, and where might its use be problematic?
- How can OpenAI tools be used responsibly in sports media to enhance journalism without replacing the human touch?
- How can we ensure that OpenAI-generated content does not perpetuate bias or misinformation in sports reporting?

Another activity we do to show that open AI can make mistakes is a verification exercise:

1 Students get an OpenAI-generated summary of a game or event, including statistics, analysis and quotes.

2 In small groups, students verify the accuracy of the OpenAI-generated report by cross-checking the information with official sources (team or league statistics, other sports journalism outlets, actual interviews with players or coaches).

3 Each group presents its findings, and we discuss challenges of using OpenAI as a source, how to spot inaccuracies, and why human oversight is essential.

4 Show students a human-written version of the same story and ask them to discuss in their teams the differences between the two articles, and which one would serve the readers better.

5 Based on what we learn in these activities, we then focus on creating a staff policy for ethics in the age of AI, by having them again review the APSE guidance on artificial intelligence. Students then write a 300–word memo to the sports editor about when and how to ethically use AI in sports reporting, including at least one ethical theory.

Ethics Keep on Coming

If we tackled all of the ethical challenges faced by student journalists covering sports, we might have another book. We can, however, do some quick hits around topics that have erupted most recently.

Brand Journalists: If you want to see what the future of college sports reporting could be, check out "Yea Alabama," the University of Alabama's new paywalled site. It has its own staff sports reporter, and serves to break the news of which some reporters can only dream. New coach hirings? They report it first. New facility? Also reported there first. What you won't see are negative stories about the Crimson Tide.

The current cost of a site like this is staggered from $5 for students to $250 for higher-end donors, but it's clear this is going to compromise the ability of journalists to cover the team competitively, and the chances of negative or even objective news content dwindle to nothing. It appears to be a model other schools are interested in pursuing.

Activity: Assign students to compare stories from in-house team platforms like "Yea Alabama" versus independent coverage. Consider what biases are visible? What stories are missing? What policies should student media adopt regarding partnerships or team affiliations?

Wanna Bet: Sports media and gambling have converged to the point that major outlets like ESPN, The Athletic, and Bleacher Report are integrating betting odds, tips and partnerships directly into their content. In college media, these dynamics create challenges few student journalists or advisers are trained to navigate. Student-athletes and anyone who works in athletics are prevented from gambling on sports that have an NCAA component, like football, basketball, or gymnastics. But it is and will continue to be a prevalent part of sports entertainment for the foreseeable future.

Key to incorporating this into your sports coverage is understanding the ethical dilemmas related to gambling. If it's so prevalent, should it be incorporated into coverage? How does it impact the athletes? We can start with identifying key tensions that would benefit from a classroom policy:

- Can student reporters cover games they've bet on?
- Should betting lines be included in student reporting?
- Is it ethical to publish "odds-focused" content if the reporter has no formal gambling background?
- Should outlets accept ads or sponsorships from betting platforms?

Next, use an anonymous tool (Google Forms) to ask students about their views on gambling:

- Do they bet on sports?
- Would they place a bet on a game they are covering?

- Would they like to post betting lines in an article?
- Would they work for a betting platform as a content creator?

Then we develop a policy in real time.

Why All of This Matters

In truth, sports media ethics deserve a book unto themselves. Anyone can learn the skills needed to cover sports, but the ethics we follow while we cover sports are the difference between acting with journalistic integrity and not. It's the difference between being a journalist and just someone who posts on sports. It's the difference between being employable and not. The codes we follow, the beliefs we uphold, the respect we provide and earn in our earliest days of sports coverage are the foundations that will hopefully help our students be positioned for long and fruitful careers. By pairing these ethical pitfalls with structured activities and discussions, students don't just learn what not to do—they begin to internalize the values that separate a sports writer from someone who simply writes about sports.

References

Associated Press Sports Editors. (2025). APSE ethics recommendations 2025. https://apsportseditors.com/apse-ethics-guidelines/

Kraft, N., & Culver, K. B. (2024). *Teaching media ethics: Integrating ethics across the mass communication curriculum*. Rowan & Littlefield.

Plaisance, P. (2024) Media ethics defined. In N. Kraft and K. B. Culver (Eds.), *Teaching media ethics: Integrating ethics across the mass communication curriculum* (pp. 1–8). Rowan & Littlefield.

Society of Professional Journalists. (2014). Society of Professional Journalists code of ethics. https://apsportseditors.com/apse-ethics-guidelines/

2 Online Course and Program Development

Brian Moritz,
St. Bonaventure University

In Spring 2020 I was teaching sports journalism at SUNY Oswego, a class I had developed and taught in-person to undergraduates for five years. But COVID-19 in mid-March forced me to move that class online. I was still teaching remotely a year later. And even with more time to build out the course, it was still very much an experiment.

In Fall 2021 I was graduate director at St. Bonaventure University and developing a graduate-level course. But the essential challenge remained the same: How do I create an online asynchronous class that is traditionally designed for and in many ways best suited for in-person instruction?

Skills-focused sports journalism classes differ from ones offered in an asynchronous online environment. They are often structured to give students the ability to learn by writing stories, discussing current events in class, covering sports on campus, and receiving frequent and substantive feedback from both peers and the instructor. This approach becomes challenging in an asynchronous online environment, where students are often scattered geographically.

But within these challenges are also opportunities.

This chapter explores those opportunities. Drawing primarily from my experiences teaching sports journalism online since 2020—first by force, then by choice as a director of online journalism MA programs—I will introduce my strategies that can help others develop a meaningful online sports journalism experience for students.

This chapter begins by addressing course development and then describes course management techniques. Consider this a collection of best practices and lessons I've learned over five years of teaching exclusively in the online space.

A few definitions to start:

- An **online course** takes place completely within a Learning-Management System (LMS) or other digital environment. While virtually all journalism classes have online components of some kind, in an online class there are no in-person meetings with students. If you are physically teaching in a classroom, this is not the chapter for you.

- An **asynchronous course** does not require students to attend at a specific day or time. Students engage with course material on their own schedule. Koo and Jiang (Koo & Jiang, 2024) define it as methods that allow instructors and students to engage and interact on their schedules within a certain time window. Asynchronous modalities normally use premade PowerPoint slides and video/audio recordings to teach key concepts that learners can access at any time (p. 2).

- A **skills course** focuses on developing specific abilities that will be useful for a student's professional career. It's usually the opposite of a lecture course, where the conveying of an intellectual ideal or branch of knowledge is the primary focus. It's a journalism equivalent of a science lab or a composition course in humanities. The goal is to know how to do a thing—in this case, report and write sports journalism stories.

Course Development

If necessity is the mother of invention, then COVID-19 was the mother of adaptation.

My professional adaptation began March 11, 2020, when all SUNY schools moved to distance learning for the rest of the spring semester (Gault, 2020). I had exactly eight days to move my in-person sports writing class online. The class remained online the following spring, as the university continued with a mix of in-person, hybrid, and online classes in the year before the population was widely vaccinated against COVID-19.

It was a challenging time, personally and professionally, for me and most others. My students in this and two other classes hadn't signed up for an online asynchronous class. I had developed a class for a full in-person classroom, not an LMS. Assignments and lectures were designed to be completed together on campus, not geographically scattered.

But as I moved to St. Bonaventure to develop asynchronous online classes for graduate students, I realized that my COVID teaching experience taught me two valuable lessons for my new job.

The first is that **an online class is not just an in-person class that has been moved to the internet.** The point is not to attempt to directly recreate the in-person experience online. This was at the root of many instructors' frustrations at distance learning during COVID, but it's impossible to recreate the vibe of an in-person class. So instead, create an experience that meets students' needs in an online asynchronous environment.

The second is that we don't have to reinvent the wheel. **A class in sports journalism is still a class in sports journalism**. The skills we are teaching our students remain the same regardless of the teaching platform—how to write compelling stories, conduct meaningful interviews, create multimedia packages, and act as ethical journalists in a diverse world. The pedagogical techniques are different because the environment is different, but the learning objectives and skills students gain remain the same.

The first step is designing the course. In the asynchronous online space, course development requires a level of intentionality and discipline. There's a rigidity to online teaching that takes some getting used to.

In developing and designing an online course, **instructors create all course content ahead of time.** Course development is more than just a syllabus, a rough outline of schedule, and vibes. Every element of your class—every lecture, video, practice exercise, assignment, rubric, discussion question for the entire term or semester—must be completed and in place *before* the class begins.

This is a best practice for online asynchronous courses because it allows for a level of quality control and is best suited for working students who may want to be able to see the entire course at once to balance their academic and professional lives. Remember, instructors in an online asynchronous course cannot show up to class with a topic and just wing it (not that any of us would ever do that), or generate discussion or work based on what is happening that day.

In online courses, learning objectives and assignment rubrics are vital. They must be clearly communicated with students each week and for each assignment. This is good practice in any class, but again, the lack of in-person contact means this is something instructors must be intentional about.

The good news is that the skills taught in asynchronous online sports journalism are the same, so the material will translate to a learning-management system. That PowerPoint on writing leads or interviewing sources can easily be turned into a short video, or a series of interactive text elements. Each LMS is different, but each one has ways to create elements that engage students rather than have them just read blocks of text. If you're lucky (as I was), your institution has instructional designers you can work with to create the material. It's best to have a mix (some videos, some reading, some interactive elements) to maximize student engagement.

Scaffolding assignments is even more important in an asynchronous class because student learning is self-paced and self-directed. Scaffolding is a pedagogical concept in which each assignment builds on what students have previously learned. It requires assignments to be given and done in a specific order, but it allows them to build towards a large goal through incremental steps. Students need to be able to build skills on top of each other more so than in person, where an instructor can provide more hands-on help during the writing process. Scaffolding also helps build students' feelings of self-efficacy (Hoermann-Elliott & Williams, 2023). In my online graduate sports journalism classes, students start with basic stories. I rely on basketball box scores[1], because I've found they are the easiest for new writers to use. Students start with the one-page box score and write a basic three-paragraph AP-style story. Then, they expand that story to 500 words. Then they receive the full game book (halftime box, final box, play by play) and write a gamer from that. Next, they get a quote sheet and work to integrate player and coach quotes in their stories. These are all posted as PDFs to the course page. A timed quiz can be given in the LMS with a box score to simulate writing on deadline.

All of this happens in the first two weeks of the course to get them used to writing sports journalism stories. Then, they move on to reporting their own stories—covering games, doing shorter features and eventually, for the final project, a long-form feature story or profile.

Here is where a potential liability of online asynchronous classes can become an asset. College campuses are a natural laboratory for sports journalism students, who can cover games and teams on campus. They usually have access to an entire athletic department's worth of players for

[1]One tip: Give students box scores from less-known or distant schools so that they cannot bring their pre-existing biases into their writing. If you use Duke-North Carolina, many students start with ideas and opinions and fandoms. Far fewer have strong feelings about Stony Brook-Binghamton women's basketball. Obviously, if you're in the America East, you should mix this up. This also gives students the chance to write about women's sports, subtly introducing inclusivity into your course.

profiles and stories for features. The geographic spread that comes from online asynchronous students obviously makes that harder.

But it's not impossible. There are high school and college sports everywhere. In my online classes, students are responsible for finding games and story ideas in their own town or area. Instead of being able to default to the sports and teams they are familiar with on campus, they're forced to do reporting and find stories in their communities.

Remember—the point is not to replicate the in-person class, but to use the online asynchronous environment work for our students.

Course Management

Course management is the biggest change for new online professors. Remember, most of the teaching content—the presentation of lessons and course material—is completed long before the start of the class. The professor's role in an online asynchronous class is less as active instructor and more as course manager.

That last word, manager, is the important one here. Once the semester or term starts, instructors have the same kind of freedom as the students do. They're not required to be in a classroom 50 minutes, three times a week. That freedom is great. It is also a challenge. Managing is a different skill than teaching.

The nature of skills classes exacerbates this challenge. Sports writing is a skill that requires a great deal of practice. Simply put, students must write a lot to learn and improve, and their instructor must provide consistent and timely feedback.

The key word to online course management is **intentionality**. Instructors need to be intentional and mindful in how they interact with students.

The main ways this is done is through message boards, course announcements, and assignment feedback. In an online course, it's critical to be responsive to students. Within reason, of course. Instructors shouldn't feel the need to be tethered to their email or to the LMS. But you create engaged students by being an engaged instructor, and in an online course, instructors need to be more intentional with their engagement.

Class discussions are the primary way students connect with each other, and the primary way that instructors will connect with students. They're often a source of frustration for instructors and students. But remember our guiding principle—we're not trying to recreate an in-person classroom, we're trying to make a great online classroom.

A great online classroom starts with a good discussion forum, which starts with good discussion questions. A good discussion question is open-ended enough to allow each student to bring their own knowledge and experience to the discussion while still being focused on that module's material.

Deadlines are an important component of developing a vibrant online course community. In my classes, each student is required to post a minimum of three times each week—an initial post by Wednesday, at least two replies to classmates by Friday. The point of the staggered deadline is to encourage conversation, replies, the kind of back-and-forth exchanges that define an engaged class. What I didn't want was students posting three times on Sunday night to get credit, but by the time they post, the week is over, and the class has moved on to a new topic and no one replies to their late comments. That kind of structure creates a culture of minimum compliance, not a community of learners.

In skills classes such as a sports journalism class, discussions are often writer's workshops. Rather than reacting to a prompt that draws from that week's readings or lessons, students are asked a writing-related question. They're asked to post potential story ideas, a draft of an assignment, ideas for multimedia elements, or to ask for help with a project. This creates opportunities for peer-editing, which helps strengthen the bond among the cohort.

A key component of creating good course discussions is for the instructor to keep their own keyboards quiet. It's tempting to respond to each post, to feel like engaging each student with each post. But I have found that nothing kills a discussion thread like too much instructor involvement. The goal is to get the students talking among themselves, and that happens when they respond and react to each other's ideas. It's important to be engaged with the discussion forums by reading them every day, but it's best not to post often. The exception is racist, sexist, transphobic, homophobic or other speech that potentially hurts other students. That should be addressed quickly and publicly.

Flower Darby, the author of *Small Teaching Online* (2019), suggests a strategy of collecting posts and responses throughout the week and then emailing the class highlights of the previous week's discussion.

This suggestion serves multiple purposes: to emphasize key points, to increase motivation by calling out individuals with exemplary posts, to serve as study guides, to ensure students don't miss something important. Done well, online discussions can be just as noisy as a lively conversation taking place in the classroom. Help students get key takeaways by summing up what they've learned, just as you do in person (p. 42).

As Darby's example shows, course announcements play a pivotal role in course management. They are a way to communicate with the entire class. I send weekly updates every Monday morning, summarizing the previous week's discussion, introducing the current week's lesson, reminding students of any due dates. Each weekly update also includes a weekly dad joke, a small way to inject a little of my personality into the online space. For sports journalism classes, class announcements can be vital ways to introduce breaking news or real-world examples into the highly structured nature of online courses. The weekly note also provides them with no excuse for missing anything.

A quick thought about Zoom or other required video-based sessions. I approach these carefully, because I think it's important for a Zoom session to have a defined purpose. You're asking people to take time off work or out of their lives to jump on a video call. A Zoom just to hang out or "be together as a group" is not responsible or respectful. St. Bonaventure offers "masterclasses" once a term, where alumni or professionals join students at all levels of graduate study. Along with the value of learning from professionals, it is a chance for students at all points in the program to see and interact with each other.

The other primary way online instructors manage a class is through grading. This is essential in a skills class such as sports journalism, where students are doing writing exercises online every week. Whether students are doing graded assignments or doing practice drills, it's important to give feedback and give it promptly. This is instructor engagement in online courses, so it matters. Give feedback promptly and give students a chance to ask questions about that feedback. Our LMS has a "feedback to learner" box, and I use that to give big-picture comments on the story. And I'll download the story as a Word Doc and do a line edit, using track changes and comments.

Yes, this is a lot of grading. No, there is no shortcut. Yes, it is worth it.

This is how instructors engage with students in an online asynchronous course. This is how students learn sports writing in an online space—by writing and getting feedback from their instructor, and by talking about it with their fellow students in an online writers' workshop.

It's not by trying to replicate an in-person classroom or newsroom.

It's about creating an online environment where students can best learn.

References

Darby, F., & Long, J. M. (2019). *Small teaching online: Applying learning science in online classes*. Jossey-Bass.

Gault, A. (2020, March). New York state takes strong steps to contain COVID-19, suspends SUNY classes, closes restaurants, and limits public gatherings. *The Oswegonian*. https://www.oswegonian.com/2020/03/12/faculty-administration-planning-for-possibility-of-online-only-classes/

Hoermann-Elliott, J., & Williams, M. (2023). Scaffolding toward Self-Efficacy: Preparing Underrepresented Writers to Pitch as Freelance Authors. *Prompt: A Journal of Academic Writing Assignments*, *7*(1). https://doi.org/10.31719/pjaw.v7i1.105

Koo, K., & Jiang, M. (2024). How Can It Really Be Effective? Experiences of Asynchronous and Synchronous Learning in Online Counseling Graduate Programs. *Journal of Educators Online*, *21*(4), 1–14. Education Research Complete. https://doi.org/10.9743/jeo.2024.21.4.17

3 **Accessible Sports Media**

Tammy Rae Matthews,
St. Bonaventure University

How do we ensure accessibility? In the context of sports media education, this is a question with many dimensions. How do we ensure that instruction is accessible? How do we teach students to produce accessible media? How do we teach students to cover athletes with disabilities? How can we take advantage of new technology to allow fans with disabilities to consume sports media?

Tackling these issues prepares students for careers in which they will have colleagues, audiences, and other stakeholders who may be neurodivergent or have physical disabilities. Sports media organizations can broaden audience reach, improve user experience, and fulfill legal responsibilities by adopting the best accessibility practices. Prioritizing accessibility—including web navigation, multimedia content, language clarity, content availability and design inclusivity—as an essential editorial standard in sports journalism, ensures that all individuals can engage with content seamlessly.

Accessibility is not a secondary concern. By sport journalism educators embracing accessibility as a core journalistic value, sports media curricula can enhance media consumer engagement. Integrating accessibility holds students accountable to the tenets of journalism.

This chapter focuses on classroom organization, accessibility standards in media production, and coverage challenges for adapted sports. It also provides a look into the future of technology designed to make media, including live sports media, more accessible to a wider range of audiences.

Accessibility in the Classroom

Best practices are just starting to emerge for accessible course design. Some things ought to be obvious: ensuring that students in wheelchairs are comfortable in classrooms and that instructors are clearly audible throughout a class space. But college and departmental policies vary depending on local codes and system policies. Moreover, students may have specific processing challenges that make it difficult for them to absorb information provided orally, such as in a lecture or via video. Instructors should consider alternative ways of providing course content that are accessible to students without compromising learning outcomes. For example, give students access to slides and notes while requiring them to create notes of their own, and always ensure that videos are captioned.

Similarly, remember that the point of evaluations is not to give students a grade but to ensure that they accomplish the learning objective for a given part of a course. Evaluations can be structured to accommodate processing challenges without diminishing the instructor's goals. Producing work under tight deadlines, for example, is a critical skill in sports media. If a student has a learning accommodation requiring that they receive extra time on assignments, allow them to produce the assignment multiple times without penalty so that they can practice speedy content creation.

Reporting and Producing Accessible Media

Interviewing

Educators should teach sports media students how to interview accessibly. This can take many forms: Reporters should offer in-person, phone, video call or text-based interviews (Watkins, 2023b). While face-to-face and phone interviews remain standard, alternative methods such as text-based, video or asynchronous communication may better suit some individuals because providing multiple options enhances accessibility and ensures more inclusive engagement (Watkins, 2023a). Ask about preferred communication methods, such as written responses for non-verbal individuals (Watkins, 2023b). Respect social distancing or mask-wearing requests (Watkins, 2023a). Ensure physical meeting locations are wheelchair-accessible and sensory-friendly (Watkins, 2023b). Inquire about preferred communication aids, such as sign language interpreters (Watkins, 2023a).

Reporters also should use plain language and simplify complex inquiries when interviewing individuals with neurodiversity (Watkins, 2023b). Offer breaks to accommodate individuals with chronic fatigue or pain (Watkins, 2023a). Provide questions in advance to accommodate different processing needs (Watkins, 2023b). Journalists should avoid making assumptions about accessibility needs and prioritize direct communication to accommodate sources effectively.

Producing Accessible Content

Sports media is not truly for everyone unless everyone can access it. Compelling stories should cater to diverse audiences, including those with auditory, cognitive, neurological, physical, speech and visual impairments. These considerations should be integral to the core principles of journalistic practice, akin to the essential elements of story production, like leads, headlines and visual content.

Sports journalism heavily relies on data visualization, infographics, charts and statistics, often lacking alternative text descriptions, making them inaccessible to screen readers. Interactive graphics must provide clear instructions for engagement (Accessibility in Media, 2025). Sporting events often feature live-streaming, which, without closed captions or transcripts, excludes individuals with hearing impairments. Certain sports news websites do not fully support keyboard navigation. Visually hidden elements can aid screen reader navigation (Accessibility in Media, 2025). Poor color contrast and design in scoreboards and game statistics make interpreting content difficult for individuals with visual impairments.

To address these issues, accessibility checklists should guide the development of media projects (Accessibility in Media, 2025). Web accessibility ensures that digital platforms, including websites, tools and technologies, are designed to accommodate individuals with specific physical or neurological needs. It helps engagement, enabling them to perceive, understand, navigate and interact with digital content. Ensuring accessibility in sports reporting allows for broader audience engagement, particularly in an era where digital consumption dominates media interactions. An example can be found at https://ft-interactive.github.io/accessibility/.

Other best practices can be adapted from the principles of search and social optimization, which sports-media professionals and students should be practicing already. Each sports news article should have a clear, descriptive title conveying the main topic. Placing the most relevant information at the beginning improves readability and searchability. For instance, "Olympics 2024: Imane Khelif's Controversy and Its Impact on Boxing" is more effective than "Breaking News: A Controversy in Boxing."

Formatting stories for ease of navigation also should be a key topic covered. Headings should structure content logically, aiding readers and assistive technologies in navigating the text. In a sports article, using headings such as "Match Analysis," "Player Statistics," and "Post-Game Interviews" ensures clarity and coherence (W3C WAI, 2025). The Associated Press does this with game stories, with specific subheads for storylines, key moments, key stats, and what happens next.

Create informative and unique page titles to structure web content for accessibility (W3C WAI, 2025). Write meaningful hyperlink text (W3C WAI, 2025). Links should use descriptive text to aid screen reader users (Accessibility in Media, 2025). They should describe their destination. Instead of vague phrases like "click here," use precise language such as "Read the full match report on the Champions League final." Similarly, journalists should offer precise instructions when directing users to live streams, scoreboards or interactive content. Instead of "Find results here," a more precise directive would be "Click on the 'Live Scores' tab to view real-time match updates." Keep content concise and readable.

Designers also should remember to implement contrast-friendly color combinations and high-contrast color schemes to improve readability for individuals with color blindness or low vision (W3C WAI, 2025). And all images and graphics should include alternative text to ensure inclusivity for visually impaired users (W3C WAI, 2025). Alt text should describe an image's purpose and the key details of the image (Accessibility in Media, 2025).

It is important to remember the difference between captions and transcriptions, both of which are important for accessibility. Captions transform spoken dialogue and auditory elements into synchronized visible text displayed on-screen for live and pre-recorded videos. Transcripts provide the non-synchronized text of spoken content, typically adjacent to video, podcast or audio materials. Unlike captions, transcripts offer the advantage of searchability (Harvard University Information Technology, 2022). Both captions and transcripts serve as critical tools in making multimedia content accessible to individuals who are hard of hearing, as well as to non-native language speakers, individuals with neurodiversity and users in noisy environments (Harvard University Information Technology, 2022).

Transcriptions and closed captions should complement all video and audio content (Accessibility in Media, 2025) to enhance accessibility for users with hearing impairments. Transcripts for interviews, commentary and press conferences should include spoken words and relevant non-verbal sounds. Captions in video content should provide correct representations of dialogue and background sounds, ensuring that hard-of-hearing audiences can fully engage with the content. Additionally, content should avoid ASCII art and special characters that disrupt screen readers, as they hinder content comprehension (Wise, 2021).

This also applies to breaking news and live updates. Ensuring accessibility requires consistently using alt-text for social media posts that describe images for screen-reader users (Wise, 2021). Social media platforms should improve accessible audience interactions, ensuring easy-to-access navigation (Accessibility in Media, 2025). Newsrooms must integrate alt-text usage into their workflow to maximize accessibility.

Accessible design (Wise, 2021) benefits audience members with disabilities and nondisabled audiences by improving content navigation, comprehension and engagement. Similar to how curb cuts and ramps facilitate mobility in physical spaces, digital accessibility tools—such as high-contrast fonts, alternative text (alt-text) for images, captions and screen-reader compatibility—enhance the experience of sports content consumers (Wise, 2021). Sports journalists must prioritize accessibility to ensure that individuals with auditory, cognitive, neurological, physical, speech and visual impairments can engage with digital content.

Ethical and Professional Considerations in Covering Adapted Sports

Students not exposed to people with disabilities may not be sensitive to how to use broadly inclusive language either in interviewing or storytelling, because people who experience disabilities are not a monolithic group (NCDJ, 2025). Journalists should avoid "the disabled," just as they would refrain from using phrases such as "the Asians," "the Jews" or "the African Americans."

Journalists should only mention a person's disability if it is relevant to the story (NCDJ, 2025). If a disability is relevant, journalists should briefly explain its significance (Associated Press, 2025a). A suitable sentence could be: "Merritt, who is blind and walks with the assistance of a guide dog, ran in the Chicago Marathon with their service animal." An inappropriate sentence would be: "Ryan, who has paraplegia, is a fan of modern art." Journalists should prioritize verification through medical sources or self-identification by the individual when referencing a diagnosis. If family members or others provide information about a disability, journalists should evaluate the source's credibility before including the information (Associated Press, 2025a).

Listening attentively during interviews allows journalists to align their language choices with the preferences of their sources. Providing interviewees with terminology options ensures alignment with their self-identification. The disability community, like other marginalized groups, has developed preferred language conventions (Watkins, 2023a). Determining the correct terminology necessitates direct engagement with sources. Language extends beyond semantics; it reflects identity and dignity. Multilingual content further enhances global accessibility for all people with disabilities and neurodiversity (Accessibility in Media, 2025).

Euphemistic language, such as "special needs" or "differently-abled," varies by cultural and linguistic context but often diminishes the lived experiences of individuals with disabilities (Watkins, 2023a). The Associated Press style guide (2025a) also says euphemisms such as "handi-capable," "differently abled" and "physically challenged" should be avoided unless explaining how someone self-identifies. Additionally, sports journalism educators should teach students not to use the terms "handicap" and "handicapped" to describe disabilities or individuals.

Certain terms carry historical and cultural stigmas. Words like "crip," "cripple," "handicap," "retarded," "idiot" and "moron" remain offensive unless reclaimed within specific disability movements (Watkins, 2023b). Similarly, function-based descriptors such as "low-functioning" and "high-functioning" often carry negative connotations (Watkins, 2023a). While some sources may self-identify using these terms, journalists must exercise discretion. Eric Garcia, an autistic journalist, stresses the importance of quoting sources verbatim while avoiding the imposition of labels that may not fully encapsulate an individual's experience (Watkins, 2023a). Sports journalists should avoid using phrases such as "he turned a blind eye" or "the group is dragging its feet" (Associated Press, 2025a). Writers should consider alternative phrasing, as words that may appear harmless to others could carry offensive or deeply personal meanings for others. Terms that suggest pity, such as "afflicted with," "battling," or "suffers from" a disability, should be replaced with neutral descriptions such as "has cancer" or "is being treated for ADHD" (Associated Press, 2025a).

Additionally, journalists should avoid mass terms such as "the blind" or "the mentally ill" in favor of more precise and individualized language (Associated Press, 2025a). Negative or condescending terminology, such as "wheelchair-bound" or "Alzheimer's victim," should be replaced with accurate and neutral descriptions like "uses a wheelchair" or "a person with Alzheimer's disease" to portray individuals with disabilities with dignity and to respect all humans in marginalized groups as they deserve (Associated Press, 2025a).

By instructing students to adopt precise, respectful and inclusive language, educators can contribute to more accurate and equitable representations of people with disabilities in sports media. The National Center on Disability and Journalism recommends neutral phrasing such as "nondisabled" or "does not have a disability" (NCDJ, 2025). AP also suggests "people without a disability" (Associated Press, 2025a). Writers should refrain from referring to nondisabled individuals as "normal" or "typical" (Associated Press, 2025a). While some governmental reports use "able-bodied," journalists should default to accurate language and avoid exclusionary implications (Watkins, 2023a). AP also instructs to avoid using "able-bodied" unless in specific government or legal contexts (Associated Press, 2025a).

Person-First versus Identity-First Language

The NCDJ guide says the phrase "disabled people" represents an identity-first linguistic approach, in contrast to people-first language, which structures phrasing as "people with disabilities" (NCDJ, 2025). Preferences vary across communities and individuals. Writers should ask individuals about their preferred terminology when discussing their disability (Watkins, 2023b). The distinction between identity-first (for example, autistic person) and person-first (for example, a person with autism) language is significant for many people, and their preferences should be respected whenever possible (Associated Press, 2025a).

Inspiration Porn

The concept of inspiration porn, popularized by disability advocate Stella Young (2014), critiques media portrayals that objectify individuals with disabilities for the benefit of nondisabled audiences. This term describes media that portray individuals with disabilities in a way that, although intended to be uplifting, reinforces the idea that disability is inherently negative. Inspiration porn infantilizes, pities, and so forth (Hegel, 1807), people with disabilities (Watkins, 2024). The AP Stylebook also reminds journalists to refrain from inspiration porn. This type of coverage often positions individuals with disabilities as objects of amazement rather than as equals (Associated Press,

2025a). Inspiration porn doesn't challenge or change societal and systemic issues. Instead, reporters should cover athletes in adapted or paralympic sports primarily as athletes, taking care to explain their backstories if doing so is relevant but to avoid making them seem heroic or glorified because of those backstories.

Innovations in Accessible Sports Media

Maintain hybrid coverage options for in-person sports events to accommodate remote audiences. Virtual participation has proven invaluable for disabled sports fans. Platforms such as Google Hangouts and YouTube offer closed captioning, though their accuracy varies (Wise, 2021). Edited transcripts post-event can further enhance accessibility. For in-person sports events, journalists should evaluate venues based on accessibility criteria, ensuring wheelchair-friendly entry points, adequate parking and accommodations for individuals with hearing impairments (Wise, 2021). Collaborating with sign-language interpreters and providing real-time captions can significantly improve inclusivity.

Although individual journalists can implement accessibility measures, systemic change requires an industry-wide commitment. Educators should encourage students to think expansively about how journalists could improve this experience. They could research up-and-coming technologies they could integrate into their work. For example, Touch2See is a touchscreen with a tactile and audio-based interface, bringing users closer to the heart of multiple sports (Touch2see, 2025). The tablet's magnetic cursor tracks the ball's position in real time, ensuring users stay engaged with the game's flow. Vibrations reflect the intensity of key moments in the match, while audio descriptions deliver precise information about the game's progression. The device automatically connects to sports data, requiring no added setup. Its intuitive design makes Touch2See easy for individuals to use without technical expertise.

Touch2See can advance accessibility in football and other sports, continuing to innovate and advocate for equal access to the emotions and excitement of live competition. The interface is available today for traditional football (soccer), rugby and basketball. The company hopes to support tennis, handball, hockey and American football (Touch2See, 2025).

All newsrooms and sports journalism require a fundamental cultural and procedural accessibility transformation within all newsrooms and sports journalism. Accessibility evaluations must reflect the audience's needs. Every educator, journalist, editor, visual storyteller and audience strategist is critical in ensuring that sports journalism remains user-friendly for people with disabilities and neurodivergent audiences. A single department cannot regulate accessibly, nor should media organizations treat it as an optional enhancement. Educators should teach students to embed it in daily journalistic and social media practices. Media organizations must secure institutional support for accessibility initiatives. Audience research should identify unmet accessibility needs to expand reach. User Experience (UX) testing should include individuals with disabilities (Accessibility in Media, 2025). Ensuring digital accessibility remains essential in providing equitable access to academic institutions' knowledge, ideas and resources to support inclusive digital environments, particularly for individuals with disabilities (Harvard University Information Technology, 2022). Educators can encourage their students to accommodate all types of sports fans and athletes in their media coverage.

Sports Journalists with Disabilities and Neurodiversity

Creating brave spaces (Arao & Clemens, 2013) in sports journalism requires consequential representation of individuals with disabilities and neurodiversity within the field. Their presence in both professional environments and educational institutions enriches the discourse and enhances coverage of disability-related topics. Sports journalists with disabilities bring essential expertise in disability reporting, including knowledge of disability language, sourcing, interviewing, data analysis and key community issues (Watkins, 2023a). Their involvement in media organizations and newsrooms should extend beyond participation to active decision-making roles.

Journalists with disabilities working in the news and media should regularly study their rights (Watkins, 2024). Resources such as the Job Accommodation Network (JAN, 2025) and the Self-Advocacy Resource and Technical Assistance Center (SARTAC, 2025) guide disclosure decisions and workplace accommodations. Self-advocacy is a foundational civil rights movement for individuals with intellectual disabilities and neurodiversity. Organizations like SARTAC (2025) equip individuals with the knowledge and skills to assert personal needs and advocate for systemic change. Effective self-advocacy involves expressing perspectives, recognizing advocacy as a universal capability, setting goals, negotiating for desired outcomes and fostering self-confidence.

Storytelling

Watkins says journalists considering covering a story about disability or neurodivergence should consider the following: Who benefits from this story? Does the narrative reinforce stereotypes or challenge them? Are voices of sources with neurodiversity and disabilities represented authentically and equitably? Are sources allowed to express their language preferences? (Watkins, 2023b). Media coverage should not confine individuals with disabilities to discussions of their conditions. People with disabilities contribute expertise across diverse fields. Journalists should include them in discussions unrelated to disability (Associated Press, 2025a).

Historically, media coverage has either excluded individuals with disabilities or presented their experiences through stereotypical narratives. Eric Garcia argues that sports journalism must recognize individuals with disabilities as part of the audience (Watkins, 2023a). By prioritizing accuracy and representation, journalists can dismantle exclusionary reporting practices. John Loeppky emphasizes that skepticism exists within the disability community due to past misrepresentations (Watkins, 2023a). One practical approach involves concluding interviews by asking sources if they have questions or concerns, thereby fostering open communication. Ugandan journalist Irene Abalo Otto highlights the importance of engaging with individuals with disabilities in their environments (Watkins, 2023a). Covering sports narratives involving athletes with disabilities, particularly those affected by conflict or displacement, necessitates accessibility considerations. Meeting sources in comfortable and accessible locations strengthens the authenticity of storytelling.

Students could also watch disability storytelling in documentaries. Filmmaker Ned Castle explores the experiences of U.S. athletes with intellectual and developmental disabilities in *All You Hear Is Noise*, a documentary that follows their journey to the Special Olympics World Games in Abu Dhabi (Frames to Life, 2023). The film captures the athletes' resilience as they navigate the pressures of international competition and the transition back to everyday life, prompting the audience to reflect on the pervasive nature of ableism in society. The documentary focuses on the intersecting journeys of three U.S. triathletes—Trent Hampton, Melanie Holmes and Chris

Wines—who train rigorously for the Games while confronting societal biases and misconceptions about their abilities. *All You Hear Is Noise* distinguishes itself by rejecting reductive media tropes often associated with intellectual disability. Rather than relying on sentimentalism or oversimplified narratives of triumph, the film presents a nuanced exploration of its subjects' experiences and fosters a deeper understanding of disability and sports.

Game Time

The semester to start educating your students about accessible sports media is the one you are in right now. Find a way to incorporate it into your existing course material. Add it to your syllabus draft for next semester. Share it with other educators. Institutionalize it.

Sports media professionals can contribute to a fairer industry by implementing accessibility-driven practices. Accessibility in sports journalism encompasses ethical reporting, all-encompassing interviewing techniques and conscious technical engagement with people with disabilities and neurodiversity. Sports media professionals can create a more immersive experience for all audiences by implementing accessible design, content structuring and multimedia adaptations. Implementing these strategies ensures that individuals with disabilities and neurodiversity can effectively access, understand and interact with sports media. By adhering to accessibility guidelines, sports journalism can uphold its commitment to fair, comprehensive and engaging sports reporting to all audiences as it evolves.

Journalism is a highly skilled field that prioritizes research and standards. Journalism's job is to uphold the integrity of the country and its industry. Journalism fosters critical critiques by asking new, powerful questions. Our unbiased veracity comes in how we report the answers to those questions. Prioritizing web accessibility is crucial in delivering those answers and quotes to the readership.

Incorporating accessibility in sports media ensures all—yes, all—sports fans can access and engage with discourse.

References

Accessibility in Media. (2025). *Accessibility in Media: Tip Sheet & Resources*. FT interactive. https://ft-interactive.github.io/accessibility/

Arao, B., & Clemens, K. (2013). From Safe Spaces to Brave Spaces: a new way to frame dialogue around diversity and social justice. In L. M. Landreman (Ed.), *The Art of Effective Facilitation: Reflections from Social Justice Educators* (pp. 135–150). Stylus.

Associated Press. (2025a). Disabilities. *Associated Press Stylebook*. https://www.apstylebook.com/ap_stylebook/disabilities?sconvid=4344

Frames to Life. (2023). *All You Hear Is Noise*. Frames to Life. https://www.framestolife.com/editorial#/ayhin/

Harvard University Information Technology. (2022, February 16). *Digital Accessibility Digest*. https://www.huit.harvard.edu/news/create-accessible-media

Hegel, G. W. (1807). *Phänomenologie des Geistes*. Suhrkamp.

JAN. (2025). Job Accommodation Network (JAN): https://askjan.org/

NCDJ. (2025). *Disability Language Style Guide*. National Center on Disability and Journalism: https://ncdj.org/style-guide/

SARTAC. (2025). *SARTAC*. Self Advocacy Resource and Technical Assistance Center. https://selfadvocacyinfo.org/

Touch2See. (2024, February 19). *Touch2See at CAN: Touch2See had the honor of deploying its tablets during the 2023 African Cup of Nations, in collaboration with CAF and TotalEnergies*. Touch2See. https://touch2see.fr/touch2see-a-la-can/

Touch2see. (2025). *Touch2see*. https://touch2see.fr/

W3C WAI. (2025). *Making the Web Accessible*. World Wide Web Consortium (W3C) Web Accessibility Initiative (WAI): https://www.w3.org/WAI/

Watkins, E. (2023a, March 7). *Guide to Investigating Disability Issues: Chapter 4— Language and Interviewing*. Global Investigative Journalism Network. https://gijn.org/?p=621285

Watkins, E. (2023b, October 19). *Language Matters: Framing the Story When Covering the Disability Community Training Recording*. YouTube. https://www.youtube.com/watch?v=-XMfRL5_WKc

Watkins, E. (2024, December 3). Journalism and Disability. *St. Bonaventure University Faculty Professional Development*.

Wise, H. (2021, October 7). *Digital accessibility is a cultural shift newsrooms need now*. Donald W. Reynolds Journalism Institute. https://rjionline.org/news/digital-accessibility-is-a-cultural-shift-newsrooms-need-now/

Young, S. (2014). *I'm not your inspiration, thank you very much*. TEDxSydney. https://www.ted.com/talks/stella_young_i_m_not_your_inspiration_thank_you_very_much

Part II
Preparing Students for Fields and Industries

4 Teaching Sports Broadcasting

Kevin Hull,
University of South Carolina

Many fans would like nothing more than to be in the stadium or arena reporting on the big game, making sports broadcasting one of the most in-demand jobs in the media. While many can speak intelligently about games, players, and strategy, being a sports broadcaster involves much more than just sitting down in front of a microphone and talking about the latest news. With that in mind, many schools are adding classes to their curriculum to address this growing interest in on-air reporting jobs. Therefore, this chapter's goal is to help instructors who are teaching one of those sports broadcasting classes.

Recommended Materials

A sports broadcasting class can be taught with a variety of different budgets. High tech cameras and full broadcasting studios can give students the opportunity to produce professional-level content that can rival most professional broadcasts. However, the same can be said for classes taught on a more reasonable budget. Therefore, the following recommended materials are basic and should allow instructors to teach those looking to learn about the field.

> **Course Textbook:** *Sports Broadcasting.* Written by Kevin Hull and published by Human Kinetics. ISBN: 9781492598572.[1] *Why this book?* This textbook was designed as a "do it all" for those looking to enter the field of sports

---

[1] This textbook is written by the chapter author. An additionally recommended text is *Total Sports Media*, written by Marc Zumoff & Max Negin, published by Taylor & Francis, ISBN: 9780429749582, 0429749589.

broadcasting. Chapters provide in-depth lessons for students, online elements give additional practice materials including video clips and tutorials, and instructors who adopt the book are provided with lesson plans, a syllabus, and answer keys for the various assessments.

Hardware: Students will need a video recording device. While some schools may already have video cameras on-site for other broadcasting classes, most beginner classes can be run with students using their smartphones. Additional purchases could include a tripod set for the phones and a basic microphone that can be plugged into the phone for better audio recording. For students who may not have a smart phone, the school may wish to purchase a set of phones that can be used.

Software: Students should have access to a video editing program. As of 2025, Adobe Premiere can be purchased with a student discount. However, most computers come with a free video editing program, such as iMovie for Apple products. In addition, some students may wish to use video editing apps on their smartphones to complete assignments.

Three Foundational Lessons in Sports Broadcasting

There are many different topics that a Sports Broadcasting class can tackle throughout the semester. The suggested textbook provides background for chapters on sports broadcasting history, the business of the industry, ethical situations, and how to find a job. For the purposes of this chapter and getting an instructor started on teaching a class in sports broadcasting, the focus will be on writing for broadcast, shooting and editing video, and social media.

Writing for Broadcast

Perhaps one of the hardest skills to teach in any broadcast class, whether it is news or sports focused, is how to write for television or radio. Since elementary school, students have been taught to write complex sentences containing multisyllabic words. However, this is almost the exact opposite of how to write for broadcast. Instead, broadcasters need to remember that their scripts are being written for the ear, not the eye. For example, a portion of a paper written for a history class can be reread if there is a section that is unclear. However, a story that is being read on a broadcast is often only heard once, so the script must be simple and easy to understand the first time for the listener.

Therefore, here are some tips to pass along to students when starting to teach broadcasting writing:

- "Write like you talk:" Ultimately this script will be read out loud, so students should write a script that is easy to speak and not just easy to read in their heads.

- "Short, simple sentences:" Broadcast sentences should be short and contain only one idea in each sentence. A sentence with more than a dozen words is likely too long.

- "Give current details:" Broadcasting is a medium in which the audience is expecting to know what is happening right now. The morning newspaper contains yesterday's news, while an evening broadcast typically focuses on the news of the day. When writing, students should focus on the aspect of the story that is still current.

- "Use active voice:" Broadcast scripts should be written in the active voice instead of the passive voice. In the active voice, the subject acts upon the verb (I threw the ball). As noted in the previous bullet point, broadcast writing focuses on what is happening now, and active voice helps to achieve that style of writing.

- "If I see it, I should hear it. If I hear it, I should see it:" For scripts that will be on television, the video is an important element of the story. Therefore, video editing and script writing should be done in conjunction with each other. If the script mentions a specific hit in a softball game, then that hit should be edited into the video. If the video is edited first and the head coach is being shown 12 seconds into the clip, then the script writer should make sure the coach is mentioned around that same time in the story.

Possible Assignments for Writing for Broadcast

Before sending students out to games or practices for their first story, instructors may wish to do some practice broadcast writing assignments. Below are three suggestions. With each assignment, students can take turns reading their scripts out loud and providing constructive criticism to classmates. This should maximize student engagement in the classroom and allow them to help each other become better writers.

- Rewrite a story from a newspaper or website. Stories from the newspaper are not formatted for broadcast, so have students find a story that is of interest to them, or select one yourself for everyone to do, and have them turn it into a 30-second broadcast script.

- Turn bullet points into a story. Provide students with a list of ten or more short bullet points about an event. The students then should take those bullet points and turn them into a cohesive broadcast script. For added difficulty, add in some facts that, while interesting, are perhaps not necessary for the story. Students will be tasked with figuring out what is important and what is not.

- Conduct a press conference. The instructor of the class can be the "head coach" of a team and can be interviewed at a press conference. Students can ask questions and then turn the information into a short script. If the session goes well, a second press conference could be arranged with an actual member of an area team.

Shooting and Editing Video

For students studying sports broadcasting, learning how to shoot both games and events can be part of the curriculum. As stated previously in this chapter, most video capturing can be done using a smart phone as technology has evolved to a point where it can often be hard to distinguish between phone video and professional video cameras. It is recommended that students use a tripod to capture video that is farther away, but it is not a necessary purchase.

Shooting Video of Games

Recording video of a baseball game is very different from getting video of a swim meet, therefore there is not a universal method to shooting games. Instead, videographers must be sure they are following the action as best they can so that the audience can get an understanding of what happened at the game. However, a few universal suggestions can be used for all sports:

- "Follow the ball:" In sports such as soccer or basketball, the easiest suggestion is to focus the camera on where the ball is and where the ball is going.

- "Use proper framing:" While following the ball is key, the camera should not be zoomed out so wide that it is difficult to see which player is which. At the same time, if the camera is zoomed in too tight, it can lead to very fast and confusing camera movements trying to follow the ball. Instead, the broadcaster should have a few players in the video frame at all times. Those shots should be close enough to be able to identify the players, but wide enough to allow for camera movement following the ball that will not be overly jarring.

- "Find a good spot:" Figuring out where to stand during the action can sometimes be just as important as knowing what to shoot. For beginners, shooting from a higher elevation than the playing surface, such as in the bleachers of a basketball game or football game, can often make the action easier to follow. From those added heights, a tripod would help keep the shots steady.

Shooting Video of Events

Not every story that a sports broadcaster reports on will be focused on a game. Instead, there are often different events that require a different type of video shooting mentality. These could include a practice, an introductory press conference, or a charitable event. For non-game stories, the goal is to make the viewer feel like they are right there at the action. To help achieve this, the following tips can be used:

- "Get lots of shots:" Instead of shooting just a few shots from the event, the broadcaster should be getting shots of anything that is of interest in the room including the people, the environment, the sounds, and anything else that can make someone feel like they are there. There is rarely such a thing as "too much video."

- "Mix up the type of shots:" In videography, the three main types of shots are a wide, medium, and tight shot. A wide shot is used to establish a full picture of what is happening at a scene. If a person is in the frame, his or her entire body is shown. For a medium shot, the videographer can zoom in slightly to show less of the person's body but see a better angle of their face. A tight shot will focus on just the main aspect of the video and will be as close as possible to the action.

- "Move around:" If possible, try to get different angles while at the event. This means the videographer should be moving around to various spots at the location, instead of simply standing in one place and moving the camera. Instead of always zooming in from far away, it is often better to physically move closer to the object to show different angles.

Editing Video

With the understanding that in-depth editing lessons can be found in various locations, including the online elements of the recommended textbook, this section will instead recommend editing tips that can be used on any platform. For highlights, a traditional 30-second highlight will start with a shot from the game that is not a play, such as the coach, the crowd, or the cheerleaders. These shots are called cutaways. After the five-second cutaway, approximately three plays will be used, traditionally ending the game highlights with the winning team doing something positive.

For events, editors should remember the phrase that was discussed in the writing portion of this chapter: "If I see it, I should hear it." If there is a script for the story, the edited piece for the event should have the video matched with those words. If the reporter is talking about something at the 15-second mark of the script, the editing should be done so that the specific thing that is being talked about will be on the screen during that time. Each shot should be no more than about five seconds but can be significantly shorter if it matches up with the script. A final event video should be about 45 seconds, with the understanding that only about the first 30 seconds or so will make the broadcast.

Possible Assignment for Shooting and Editing Video

The best way to work on shooting and editing video is to practice as much as possible. For a class session, the instructor may split the class into two groups. The first group will "play a sport"—something as simple as throwing a crinkled-up piece of paper in a classroom or kicking a soccer ball back and forth outside – while the second group will shoot video of them. At the halfway point of the class, the two groups switch roles. In the next class, everyone will be responsible for editing a 30–45 second video piece.

For game footage, a low stakes opportunity to practice shooting video for highlights could be attending an intramural sporting event. After getting clearance from the campus recreation, students should shoot a game and then come back to the classroom to edit together a 30-second highlight package. In both assignments, the instructor should be ensuring that the action is easy to follow, proper shooting and editing technique is being used, and that an accompanying script matches up to what is being shown on the screen.

Social Media

While most of the duties of a sports broadcaster focus on their on-air responsibilities, the emergence of social media has added additional tasks to the daily to-do list while working. Sports journalists are now expected to give updates immediately on these social networks, instead of simply waiting until the morning newspaper or the late television news. Therefore, it is no surprise that many media outlets require their journalists to be on one (or more) of the platforms.

The constant evolution of social media networks makes it difficult to provide platform-specific tips. For example, Instagram started as a photo-sharing app, but many now use it primarily for video, so the "best practices" have evolved since it began. Instead of attempting to provide tips, here are some of the ways in which students can be taught how to use social media when learning to be sports broadcasters:

- "Delivering news updates:" The first method of delivering news updates would be straightforward sports news. This could include hirings, firings, injury updates, player updates, and team information.

- "In-game updates:" Another way to deliver news is to provide updates on games as they are happening. This can be especially effective for games that are not on television or radio. Social media allows journalists at the games to send frequent updates about what is happening.

- "Audience engagement:" Interaction with followers can happen in a variety of ways, such as answering questions, asking the audience for its opinion, or simply injecting themselves into viewer conversations.

- "Promotion:" One of the aspects of social media that is appealing for broadcasters is the ability to promote their work. Some social media platforms allow direct links to be placed within the messages that are being sent, so followers can easily go directly to the website for the complete story.

- "Get it right:" It should go without saying that an important part of the job, whether in social media or on the air, is making sure the facts are correct. Social media has created a rush to be the *first* to report the news, and that sometimes can lead to mistakes. Students should be taught that it is more important to be correct on social media than it is to be first.

Possible Assignment for Social Media

Before sending students out in the field to work on social media assignments, some practice activities can be done in the classroom. Three possible assignments include:

- "What the pros are doing:" Students should pick a sports broadcaster that they admire and review his or her social media accounts. They should examine the last 25 posts and see how that broadcaster is using social media. Students in the class can then compare answers based on the different jobs, employers, and expertise to see how they are the same or different.

- "Big game review:" Pick a recent sporting event and review as a class how various sports broadcasters and television networks used social media during the event. Students can discuss what they might continue to use and what they would have done differently.

- "What if?" Pick a sporting event that happened before social media began in the year 1997. For that sporting event, students should act as sports broadcasters and create an entire social media portfolio consisting of messages from various platforms.

Final Classroom Assignment

A final assignment in this class can be an all-encompassing project addressing the lessons learned so far in this chapter. Students can attend a game or event where they shoot video, write a script, edit the video, and send out social media updates from the game/event. Students can update their final video to a video sharing service or a classroom Dropbox. If time allows, the edited videos can be watched in class, giving students the opportunity to celebrate their successes and see what their classmates completed.

5 **Beyond Media Relations**
Sports-Relevant Public Relations Skills

Betsy Emmons,
University of Nebraska-Lincoln

Public relations is an applied degree that includes a foundation of media and journalism knowledge along with strategic planning, content creation, and study of communication environments. The industry is often confused with marketing. As Broom and Sha (2013) note in their update to popular public relations textbook *Effective Public Relations*, the field is understood less by what it is than what it does. Public relations is best accomplished when the public is the priority; marketing's main work is in transactional spaces. While crossover inevitably occurs, especially in converged media spaces, public relations serves distinct organizational goals (L'Etang, 2006).

While sports journalism and sports broadcasting tend to be more visible paths to careers in sports communication, sports public relations is far less understood and can be more confusing to explain (Emmons, et al., 2025). Sports public relations includes elements of media work but also includes specialized areas such as social media content creation, event management, non-profit outreach, media training, and sponsor relations. These strategic processes are separate from traditional media relations that is the most top-of-mind aspect of sports public relations.

This chapter notes key sports public relations skill development areas helpful for incorporation in a sports public relations course sequence or program.[1] While media relations remains a cornerstone of sports PR professional development, related sports-specific aspects are important to offer other crucial areas of study in sports public relations. Sample class topic ideas are included in each sub-section to apply learning areas in practice.

---

[1] Stoldt, et al.'s 2021 textbook *Sport Public Relations* and Coombs and Harker's 2022 text *Strategic Sport Communication* are two useful resources for academic study in sports public relations.

Media Relations—An Important Foundation

The media relations function is a highly visible primary public relations role in organized sports (Boyle & Haynes, 2014). Press conferences, game notes, statements, press releases, media guides, pre-season media days, and media centers keep strategic communications professionals actively engaged in media relations. Skill development in these tactics will directly benefit a sports public relations student.

Writing Skills

Written tactic skill development is crucial for sports communicators. This is one of the key areas of value in public relations education and where the value of media education in public relations is useful. Even with artificial intelligence, real-time game play and interpretation will inevitably require human involvement and oversight.

Teaching "what is news" and the six attributes of newsworthiness, along with inverted pyramid news writing and Associated Press (AP) style, are key for public relations writing. The fundamentals of press releases are necessary for PR professionals to know. Statements and media advisories, from writing them to distributing them, are likewise necessary foundations for PR-centric work. Sports media kits and media guides are vital resources that are usually produced periodically per season and provide key insights to the media about personnel and players. Game notes are indispensable as communication resources, as they provide necessary aggregate data in easy-to-use formats, and have broad applicability for use. Game notes take the media guide information and propel it into game-by-game information, offering media quick access to team news. They tend to be printed documents, even in the digital era, as print documents are easy to draw upon in the moment during games.

Class Idea: Review media guides for your university's teams. Note components that would be helpful for members of various media when reporting about the teams.

Media Credentials and Media Centers

One of the most crucial parts of the in-person, simultaneously mediated sporting event is the media credential system. Media credentials are identification badges worn by members of media while attending ticketed or controlled-access events, including sporting events. Since the media work in protected areas, such as on fields, in locker rooms or preferred-seating areas, access must be both limited and monitored. While not often studied, walking students through how media credentials are requested and given are worth practice activities and course discussions. In a freelancer, social media influencer and entrepreneur media space, considering the number of media on a court or field or within locker rooms or event workspace is important (Hermes, et al., 2014). Digital media groups and other non-legacy media are parts of sporting event storytelling, but not all requests can, or should, be honored.

Media center preparation generally falls into the public relations function. Media centers are designated areas inside sports venues where print and digital-based journalists are able to report on games. Photographers and social media content producers may also use the space, although they are generally near the field of play during the event. Broadcasters and radio productions often have their own media suites. Media centers tend to be in the areas where game notes and press information are available along with workstations and charger outlets. Pre-emptive thinking by a wise PR pro for these and other anticipatory needs such as safe storage for personal items and refreshments makes for a seamless experience and good PR.

Class Idea: Brainstorm a list of requirements for a media center so that all types of media are able to work efficiently during an entire sporting event.

Press Conferences

Press conferences are a main aspect of mediated sports and are another important sports public relations function. Media access to coaches, athletes, and athletic staff is often through press conferences. Media contracts for professional sports usually include required interviews with the sports organization's stakeholders, particularly athletes and coaches, which is why the inevitable halftime and post-game reports happen.[2] Post-game press

---

[2]The Professional Football Writers of America website explains one such policy from the National Football League—its media access policy promises post-game and other media access (NFL Media, 2024).

conferences are a regular feature of mediated sports and often broadcast live or streamed to social media platforms.

Preparation for press conferences includes allocating time and space, usually a multi-media friendly room, to be set up for pre-game, post-game or event week press conferences. An understanding of lighting and color themes for photography, branded items such as sponsor beverages available with visible labels and step-and-repeats with team and sponsor logos are fundamental parts of press conferences that assist with both promotion and marketing efforts. When a sport is in season, regular press conferences such as a weekly coach's press conference can be common. Player availability days are also common. Depending on the event, pre-game press conferences occur on multiple days leading up to games to allow access to various stakeholders. Championship games are one such environment—media are interested in pre-event quotes to build story lines and generate content well before game day.

Class Idea: Try a mock press conference. Divide students into roles, including athletes and coaches to be interviewed and various media roles. Prepare the physical space for the press conference.

Sports Public Relations Roles—Evolving and Diverse

In-House Reporter Roles

In converged modern sports media, an in-house reporter writes team news alongside journalists. The role is at its core a public relations function, as writing for the team's owned media is promotional work. For this role, the same aspects that help define journalistic writing, such as the inverted pyramid writing format and AP style, apply. Similarly, quote attribution, source citing, relevant photos and video content are journalistic practices applied in a public relations context to offer team and athlete information for stakeholders of all types—fans, journalists, or even athletes to amplify on their own social channels.

Class Idea: Attend a unique game on campus—try an intramural game or sports tournament. Have students write game recaps immediately after the game appears on the university's website. Choosing a less-covered sport is a great way to stretch sports knowledge.

Social Media in Sports Organizations

Social media has grown to be a main communication function for sports organizations. For the sports public relations professional, depending on the size of the organization, social media might be a part of the job or is its own job, with a title of "content creator" or "social media specialist." Many have argued that social media were afterthoughts in sports organizations, but now, in larger organizations, content for social media is often (but not always) a dedicated job role. Awareness of the role of social media, some specialized access and an understanding of best practices for various platforms are helpful skills to teach new sports communication professionals doing social media work.

Class Idea: Research a team on popular video-centric social media (Instagram, TikTok or YouTube). Review account following, posting frequency, tagging, brand voice, and other elements. Then, create a post that might appear on the team's account using best practices.

Event Management

Games, matches and other competitive endeavors are sporting "events" in themselves, and the various roles match the needs of the cycle of home games and away games as the season goes on. However, there are also a myriad of special events involved in organized sports that go beyond the season's work or are opportunities unto themselves. These include charity events, special days (signing days or events for sponsors, for example), ribbon-cuttings and other community partnership options, brand activations, and more. Events can be split among marketing, sponsorship, community relations and communication roles, and depending on the size of the sport can be their own role. There are also career opportunities in event management—large scale sporting events such as The World Games or Ironman races require months of logistical planning with several moving parts and multiple mini-events that surround the main action.

Sporting events are great applied learning opportunities for undergraduate student sports communication/PR courses. Having students implement events from start to finish is deeply rewarding and emphasizes skills that will help in multiple aspects of a sports communication role. Some ideas for classroom activities include asking students to come up with sporting event ideas for non-profit or charity partners. They might also move toward developing complete plans, working with an established group to implement a sports-related event (such as a 5k run or opening day with a local youth sport league), or re-imagine a well-known event with a proposal, such as for a fan day or homecoming week. Sporting event projects are often good fits for campaign courses or upper-level sports communication courses, but a scaled version could be taught in an intermediate level course.

Another opportunity for sporting event management experience is to check for opportunities with unique events in the local area. For example, high school state sports playoffs and championships might occur near the university, or even college-level events such as conference playoffs. Special event teams are generally in place but might have volunteer opportunities available—even participating in venue preparation or media center upkeep teach valuable lessons about how such sporting events operate. The best practice is on-site.

Class Idea: Look at a team's website for any brand activations or brand partnership events. Discuss what the preparation for such events would entail, and what Return On Investment (ROI) would be expected for both the brand and the team.

Strategic Public Relations—Areas of Thought Leadership and Counsel in Sports Community Partnerships

Community Relations

The community relations role is responsible for working with non-profit groups, civic organizations, and the government to nurture positive and beneficial interactions. This is an area where sports public relations courses can also use experiential learning.[3] Having students brainstorm non-profit groups that could partner with sports organizations for events, fundraising opportunities, or awareness endeavors can be helpful ways to incorporate classroom tactics into strategic plans. Finding mutually beneficial ties is ideal and demonstrates the goal of community relations work. It is important to remember that sports organizations should be good members of the communities they represent, and community relations can highlight

---

[3]Experiential learning is defined as active application of course skills. Real projects or fieldwork with sports-adjacent clients are often used.

involvement. Examples include non-profits such as cancer awareness groups highlighting a member of the sports organization able to speak about the non-profit's purpose.

Class Idea: Choose a sport with a local team. Then, review a local directory, find a non-profit advocacy group to partner with. Explain why the partnership would work. Create a specific partnership activity with the purpose of the non-profit group at the core with team support.

Sponsor Relations

Corporate sponsorships are often tied to marketing and sales but have significant crossovers into public relations. Students gain valuable experience considering sponsor relations as well as the enormous funding behind corporate sponsorships that generate organization revenue. A large corporation's financial investment in a sports organization includes several contractual obligations that include relationship building. These can include access to athletes and coaches at events, other events such as hospitality suite meet-and-greets, special ticketed days, souvenirs, and more.

Sports sponsorship continues to grow as businesses see the reciprocal benefits of sponsor partnerships. Teaching a module on typical sponsorship contracts and what activities a PR professional might assist with or lead would be practical introductions to the sponsorship aspect of sports.

Class Idea: Visit a sports venue in person. Note the banner ads and other in-venue advertisements. Discuss what relationship-building activities the venue's teams might assist with for sponsors to support the financial investment. See places on-site where the sponsorship may serve reciprocal purposes to be aware of (a soft drink sponsorship requiring only that brand for sale in concessions, for example).

Name, Image and Likeness

The Name, Image and Likeness (NIL) opportunities that have created more student-athlete promotion opportunities have likewise created sports PR opportunities. As of this chapter's writing, NIL is evolving, but promotion work nonetheless is important. NIL collectives at many universities offer appearance fees and promotional fees for athletes. Sports PR professionals help formalize opportunities and serve as on-site leadership for appearances as well as content management and assistance with media partnerships.

NIL appearances include opportunities at charity fundraisers, sales events, and other activities. After fees are paid for player appearances, there is sometimes no formal direction at the event for what players are supposed to do. Asking student-athletes to interact with donors, fans, and business leaders can be awkward; a sports PR professional serves a helpful role in facilitating activities, coaching athletes on appearances, and working with sponsoring groups for a positive experience for all.

Class Idea: Brainstorm an in-person student-athlete appearance at a local car dealer sales day. How long should the athletes be there? What should they do? What is the beneficial outcome for the car dealer? How can a PR professional assist with preparing the athletes and the dealership for a smooth event?

Media Training

Formal media training is helpful for most roles in a sports organization but especially for young and developing athletes and coaching staff. Generally, working with the media gets better with experience—mock interviews can help interview subjects improve their camera presence. Offering interview questions is another way to help interview subjects anticipate topics and think through answers before an interview. Basic media activities like 30-second athlete introduction videos are easy to do and allow camera experience. Practice interviews after difficult situations and setbacks as well as wins are useful.

Class Idea: In groups, students serve as both interview subjects and interviewers; have a camera operator and interview observer. Record the interviews live. Then, review the interview videos to reflect on what was done well and what could be improved upon.

Conclusion

The areas of sports public relations mentioned here work well for intermediate level courses and serve as an introduction for upper-level courses or niche courses (a social media in sports course, for example). Areas of public relations counsel and management such as issues management, government relations and public affairs, reputation management, crisis communication, corporate social responsibility, and campaign management are beyond the scope of this chapter but are worthy continuations of the foundational areas presented here. There is much opportunity in sports PR; this chapter notes basic highlights.

Given the converged co-creation media space that sports occupy, the sports PR professional's role will continue to evolve. The need for professional communication will not cease, and thus there is much career opportunity in a sports PR role. Growing public relations skill development in sports communication programs will be important, and program directors should be sure that PR skill development sits in equal steed with other sports media skill development.

References

Boyle, R., & Haynes, R. (2014). Sport, public relations and social media. In *Routledge Handbook of Sport and New Media* (pp. 133–142). Routledge.

Broom, G., & Sha, B. (2013). *Cutlip and Center's Effective Public Relations (11th ed.).* Pearson.

Coombs, W. T., & Harker, J. L. (2022). *Strategic Sport Communication.* Routledge.

Emmons, B., Hull, K., & Petrotta, B. (2025). "The Employment landscape has shifted massively, and we must shift with it:" A review of sports public relations courses within sports communication programs. AEJMC 2025 Conference Proceedings, San Francisco, CA.

Hermes, J., Wihbey, J., Junco, R., & Aricak, O. (2014). Who gets a press pass? Media credentialing practices in the United States. *Media Credentialing Practices in the United States (June 5, 2014). Berkman Center Research Publication* (2014–11).

L'Etang, J. (2006). Public relations and sport in promotional culture. *Public Relations Review, 32*(4), 386–394.

Stoldt, G. C., Dittmore, S. W., Ross, M., & Branvold, S. E. (2021). *Sports Public Relations.* 3rd Ed. Human Kinetics.

6 Teaching Sports Marketing to Media Students

Candy Lee, Northwestern University

Students usually think that sports marketing is about teams and leagues wanting more consumers to attend a game. Although that is a part of what sports marketing is about, it is also about how organizations use the world of sports to attract clients and customers to buy their products. It is also about how the media uses sports to entice brands to showcase their products. It is also about events, social media, AI, sponsorship, crisis and celebrity handling, social purpose too, all focused through the lens of sports.

A sports marketing instructor usually has students who like sports but need more in-depth knowledge of marketing, such as sponsorship or the growth of women's sports. Students need to understand branding and positioning, but the class activities and homework are about sports.

Sports marketing generally works in an integrated marketing communications environment because students will benefit from being knowledgeable in insights, financial planning, marketing, media, and consideration of goal setting. Thus, the overlay of sports onto the integrated marketing communications mindset will benefit the teacher in planning the syllabus.

Sample Introduction to a Class Syllabus

Sports marketing is nuanced. It may mean how a team is marketed, but it may also mean how a soft drink uses a team to reach its audience. It may encompass why an insurance company views sponsoring a tournament as value or how a car company thinks about endorsing a celebrity. Sports marketing runs the spectrum from crisis communication on a social issue connected to a celebrity behaving badly to how to price tickets when a favorite player suddenly announces retirement at the end of the season. Sports marketing is an opportunity to use sports—and indeed entertainment—to explore some important marketing concepts that are utilized in many areas under the umbrella of sports. The students will be able to demonstrate and apply concepts to address marketing and communications challenges to analyze how marketing plays a role in sports. Students may be encouraged to take a course in sports marketing, or a teacher might add an overview on the subject within a journalism course or communications course, for several reasons:

- Distinguish the different kinds of marketing that exist within sports, from experiential to celebrity
- Rationalize marketing decisions, considering challenges and opportunities in the context of sports
- Analyze the role of sports marketing in reaching and growing an audience.

Structure and Scope

Some aspects of this kind of course resemble a traditional marketing class, such as branding and positioning. Specific areas, such as sponsorship, are more emphasized because of their importance to sports organizations. However, students in sports marketing develop special relationships with traditional subjects such as branding. Players now carry logos on uniforms, so there are brands of products sitting on brands of people within brands of teams within a brand of a stadium within the brand of a league. Thus, sports marketing may be viewed through a different lens in the brand telescope.

The other potential area to be discussed is how sports think about competition. Most students will think that the potential competition for a game is another game on that night, possibly on TV or in town, because the students usually are sports fanatics. The real competition, however, is anything that the potential viewer could spend time and money on: a dinner out; play with children; a nap; binge-watching a show; a comedy club; or any other event in town.

Instructors can arrange the following in the order that suits the style of the class and topics that are appropriate for subject matter (for example, if a game is in town).

Part A: Traditional Marketing Knowledge

This section discusses marketing knowledge related to branding and positioning, marketing objective, the "5 P's," and uses of social media and artificial intelligence. These are topics that are in the realm of traditional marketing but the lens used is within the sports world.

Branding and Positioning

A brand is a name given to a product, service, place or person, and the purpose is to provide identification, ensure legal protection, add differentiation from others, and ensure information, creating something unique. Brands can be personified by trademarks, logos, slogans, and ads. Brands seek to convey a story, such as Volvo meaning safety to people, or Dove associating its soap with normal body types instead of traditional models, celebrating "real beauty."

Brand equity is the value one gives to the brand, especially when that value is higher than the realizable asset. For example, if students want a cola at Walmart, will they pay more to buy Coca-Cola over the store brand? Most will say yes. The higher cost represents both a psychological and economic brand equity in Coca-Cola because we have imbued Coke with a value.

Class Activity: Ask the students if they are a brand? Ask those that say "yes," why? Ask those that say, no, why? Then ask if LeBron James is a brand? Why?

Positioning is locating the brand in relation to its competitors and ensuring that its attributes are defined. To do that, the students need to fill out a positioning statement that provides a differentiating benefit: To (target market), (brand) is the (competitive frame) that provides (differentiating attribute, benefit or image). An example: To *office workers*, **Fedex** is the *brand of express delivery service* that provides *guaranteed on-time delivery*.

Class activity: Have the students do a positioning statement for ESPN. Example: For **sports fans**, **ESPN** is the *media platform* that provides *sports programming globally.*

A positioning map is drawn on X and Y axes where the student inserts the attribute tags for each end of each axis in order for the brand to be in the top right-hand corner. To consider a positioning map, students should think about:

- What type of item is it? Is it a product such as a sweatshirt or is it a team? Or is it a drink such as Coca-Cola or Gatorade?

- Who are the main competitors and list them? Maybe go to a store and look.
- What are the key attributes to compare? Students may sometimes think very subjectively about things such as taste, but it is good to steer them to areas that are quantifiable, such as price, quality, performance, innovation, brand prestige.
- Who is the target market? Age and other demographics might be appropriate here, but also there might be junior athletes or coaches, and so forth.

As an example: a group of friends go to Orlando for the weekend and are looking for an activity for the evening. Do a positioning map for the NBA's Orlando Magic as the top choice for the group of friends. The axis coordinates might be "group appeal" and "entertainment" or they might be "sports theme" and "ease of talking together." Students select what is on the axis coordinates, but they have to have the Magic in the top right corner and then put the competition such as restaurants, theme parks, nightclubs, music venues in

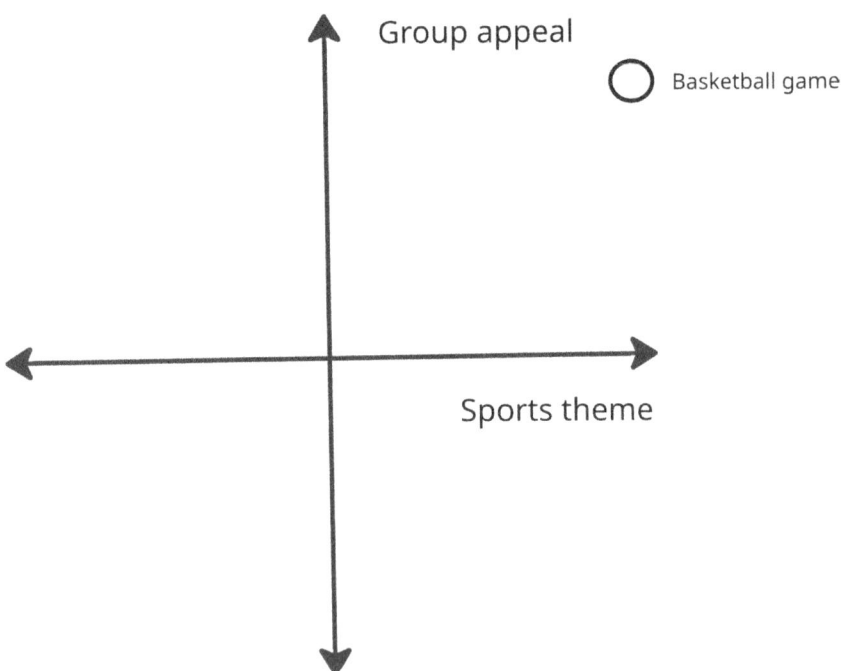

Figure 6.1 Brand Positioning Map.

the other quadrants. Students can generically bunch all theme parks under a generic name such as nightclubs or individually name them such as Disney and Universal. The point is for students to understand the concept of competitors for a product or service and figure out what attributes create the best differentiation for the specific product/service for which they are doing the positioning map.

Class Activity: Have students create a positioning map as an exercise to understand competitive analysis. I give them the choice of doing a positioning map for Gatorade or Air Jordans or for a team of their choice. They must put the tags on the two axes and then place the competition where their product would end up in the top right-hand corner. For example, if they did Gatorade, the coordinates might be price and electrolyte content, and the competitors might include Propel, Bodyarmor, coffee, and tea.

Objectives for Marketing

The organization will have set a goal (or several) for the year ahead, and marketing has to set goals that align to achieve the overall goal. For example, the organization's goals might be to double revenue. Marketing goals might be to launch two new products that will achieve this additional revenue. Marketing will state the goal and also will include a measurement so it is clear to all how to know if the goal has been reached by a certain date. Thus, it is important that objectives include a timeline, with interim markers that must be met.

The objectives or goals should be SMART (Lawler & Hornyak, 2012):

- S is for Specific. The goal or objective has to be clearly defined so all understand what needs to occur.

- M is for Measurable: Each objective must be capable of a result that is known for a conclusion. You don't want to penalize well conducted research or testing that does not work. If you do, you might stifle innovation. But you do want to ensure some bar to be certain that each idea or campaign is capable of an outcome that proves a result.

- A is for Achievable. The objective should stretch the team, but it should be within the realm of possibility. If the team has found 5,000 customers for a product and then says it will sell a million units, it is hard to understand how the objective is achievable.

- R is Relevant. The objective should be worthwhile for your team to spend time on it and resources to be allotted to it. The objective means you will not be spending time on other items. You can explain the idea of sunk costs and opportunity costs for this letter (R).
- T stands for Time-bound. All objectives need to be time-bound, ensuring the team understands the plan and the timeline.

Class Activity: Your favorite team wants to increase its ticket sales. Create SMART goals for the team by brainstorming within groups. Each group should consider each aspect of the SMART goals and then share their findings.

The Five Ps

Early marketing in the 1970s and 1980s discussed the four Ps: Price, Promotion, Placement, Product (Goi, 2009). Since then, there has been a tendency to not talk about them because the fifth P, People, was omitted. All marketing needs to be audience-centric, so leaving out people is now thought to be suspect. However, what was behind the 4Ps still needs to be understood by all students.

Product

- What type of product is this brand and what are the benefits?
- What does it look like? Logo? Packaging? What are the features?
- What are any warranties and service considerations?
- Extensions to the product (think swifter and sheets)
- What are the kinds of inventory demands and logistics with stocking?

Promotion

- What kind of advertising to do?
- What segmentation do you do on your customer base? Will you do one-to-one marketing? At the point of sale? Any specific kind of merchandising?
- Any incentives to the customer or sales force or influencers to buy/use?
- Any public relations?

- How do you plan to acquire and retain customers?
- Do you go full out with your ideas, or do you test with a small group before?
- What about customer service?
- What is the role of legal review in ensuring your promotion is above board?

Place

- Where are you distributing?
- Do you use retailers? Do you use wholesalers? Are you planning on business-to-business?
- What kind of inventory do you need to have on hand and how do you plan on restocking?
- If hosting your own site, how do you run your e-commerce site?
- Will you offer more items after your customer has selected so that you upsell/cross-sell?

Price

- Recommended price/ensuring your margin
- How and when payments will be made?
- How will refunds be made?
- Will you have credit terms? Taking credit cards?
- Bundling with other items/having special terms for B2B.

Class Activity: Have your class create a team merchandise item and then apply the 4 Ps to selling that item. Have them work in groups and then present their findings to the class at large. Each group selects the team and the merchandise item and considers the bullets under the 4 Ps and what is required to have the item be sold successfully.

People

It is always worth returning to the concept that marketing is about the customer. Even though the original 4 Ps did not include People, all marketing is centered on the customer, client or audience. What motivates them? Why would they be willing to give you their time, energy, money, thought? What insights have you gleaned about your audience? What pain points do you want to solve?

Use of Social Media and Artificial Intelligence

Since most students have used social media nearly all their lives, they feel immediately drawn to social platforms to draw fans. Often the students skip the goal setting, target audience, and measurement to immediately create a list of social tactics for any exercise. Using AI sometimes helps, but I want to ensure that they verify anything created with large language models. Whatever the assignment, I always start off by asking what the overall goal is, who the target audience is, and what pain points are addressed. I also sometimes ask for a competitive analysis. Then I let them loose on tactics.

Have students design social tactics that support the objectives that are created and explain how the tactics relate to an objective. The biggest misalignment usually is the creation of an overall strategy/objective with a list of tactics that do not line up to support that objective. Social content concepts can be real-time updates on the fans or by the fans and highlighted by marketing. Showcasing user-generated content has a dual purpose: The marketing team does not have to create everything, and fan engagement in contests and outcomes grows. Social media can show behind-the-scenes material or offer insights into the game. Many teams have causes, and social media can help promote the sense of purpose that the players and team have shown a commitment and passion to encourage support among fans.

For artificial intelligence use, have students open up an AI platform and consider tools for integration into sports. AI models can predict outcomes on historical data, so it can help forecast sales and merchandise trends. Generative AI can generate engaging content concepts for social media, including videos and social media posts. Be sure to tell the AI which social platform is being used so the length and picture fit. AI can also look at data for insights into fan behavior so that inventory for food, or future consumer management can be improved.

Class Activity: If you as a teacher can get access to a team's ticket or merchandise sales, ask students to use AI to analyze future trends, and then present marketing strategies based on their findings. The students could also segment the audience and design specific communication messages for each portfolio.

If you do not have access to data, ask the students to:

- *Use AI to design social messages*
- *Use historical data to predict outcomes of matches*
- *Create a highlight reel generation of a game*
- *Use AI to explore the ethics of using AI. Have the students form groups pro and against.*

Part B: Financial Underpinning

General Business and Marketing Planning

Marketers plan with numbers all the time because they budget; acquire customers; spend on campaigns; measure success. They can work from historical figures with an index for the current year or budget from scratch. Students should understand variable costs: a cost that varies with sales volume; fixed costs: business costs, such as rent, that are constant whatever the quantity of goods or services produced. They should understand that they might outsource some work to an agency and pay a commission, or perhaps a retainer with a fee.

Pricing

It helps if students have a basic understanding of how markets and pricing work. If students have not taken an introductory course in economics or in business, then instructors should be prepared to cover some basics. Most people decide pricing by looking at all the costs involved and then deciding how much margin they need and adding that on top. However, corporations determine prices based on supply, demand, and elasticity. Price skimming is when the product starts high and then drops, but early adopters are willing to pay a premium: iPhones being the perfect example. I always ask who buys the newest iPhone early and there is always someone. Penetration pricing is setting the price low enough to get the market as full of the product as possible. Prestige pricing ensures that the market recognizes luxury. Price elasticity of demand is the economic measure of the change in the quantity if the price changes. Inelastic means that the product is insensitive to price changes; gasoline is usually considered inelastic because we keep driving even when fuel prices rise. Super Bowl commercials seem to be inelastic because they seem to sell out even when the prices seem very high!

Dynamic/Variable Ticket Pricing

This is pricing for different times/seasons/audiences. We are used to sitting on an airplane next to a person who paid a different price. At sporting events, prices vary on a Tuesday in April versus a Saturday in August; if in the sunshine or shade; if against a big rival or a perennially losing team. Ticket prices also change if a major player announces retirement halfway through a season.

Class activity: Charlotte is bringing in a baseball team and you are the new owner. I go to the white board and with the students create two fields: one is all the ways an owner will receive revenue. The other is all the ways that the owner will incur costs. The students think of many ways but not all, so I remind them of costs such as practice facilities or travel to away games. I have made a sheet of the revenue and costs so that when they are divided up into groups of four or five to discuss, they each have a sheet to refer to. I ask students to mark the percentages earned from the following in revenue and the percentages that they think it will cost them. Both percentages must add up to 100%

- *Revenue: tickets; merchandise; sponsors; broadcast; concessions; parking; outside events and anything else the students think of*
- *Costs: Travel; agencies; maintenance of stadium; salaries of players; coaches; crew; cost of tickets; branding events; practice facilities; equipment; social responsibilities; database analytics; sales folks; credit card fees; insurance; and anything else the students think of.*

We think of the revenue and costs together on the white board and then in groups they allocate the percentages and then we compare. The students find this exercise one of the most revealing of the year, because they suddenly realize how hard it is to make all the decisions relating to the team. Usually marketing gets too little because it is hard to give it very much and still allocate monies for everything else.

Part C: Sport Orientation Marketing

Inconsistent Products and Loyalty

Think of drinking a bottle of Coke. You have the same experience every time (unless you have too many), and Coca-Cola's consistency is a selling point. But a game is different every time. This makes a game an inconsistent and intangible product. When products are inconsistent, logos become very important because there is no easy representation of the actual product. When we think of Travelers or Prudential Insurance, we may mentally see an umbrella or a rock, because their marketers know we cannot visualize insurance. A logo stands in not only for the intangible and inconsistent product, but also for all the history that has inspired fans to remain loyal to the product. Similarly, logos in sports stand in for teams.

Loyalty programs have grown in the sports field. When teams offer fans benefits for remaining loyal, such as allowing longtime season ticket holders to choose better seats, they gather data that can be used for fan engagement. The data is vital so that customer retention for ticket sales and fan experience can be maximized. Teams have built loyalty programs to retain fans to ensure that support stays stable even during losing seasons or to thwart any downturns. Manchester United and the Dallas Cowboys are good examples of loyalty programs that have retained fans despite the lack of sustained success in recent years. Another example is betting sites such as Caesars, BetMGM, DraftKings, or Fanatics: They invest heavily in customer retention.

Class Activities: Students can compare loyalty programs and draw conclusions about what successful and less-successful teams do to retain fans, or they can design one for a team of their choice.

Sponsorship

Sponsorship is the financial or in-kind support of an activity used primarily to reach business goals. The sponsor should enumerate promotional objectives such as these:

- Increase brand awareness
- Enhance image/shape consumer attitudes
- Drive sales
- Create positive publicity/heighten visibility
- Differentiate from competitors
- Help with good "Corporate Citizen" role
- Enhance business, consumer and VIP relations.

The key to a successful sponsorship relationship is the ability to align brand values, strengthen brand image, propagate brand loyalty, leverage marketing strengths, and pool available resources. Sponsorship rights can include the right to use a logo or a trademark, the right to use phrases such as "official sponsor," the right of service (Coca Cola pouring rights, for example), the right to exclusivity, the right to an event or hospitality, or the right to activities such as contests. Rights are negotiated for exclusivity and for pass-through. The latter means that the rights holder has the right to provide the sponsorship to another. An example would be: Home Depot has the rights to the event, but Miracle-Gro has pass-through rights, and both entities can sponsor a joint contest.

Class activity: Divide the class into groups and have each group design a new sponsorship for a team or league.

Event Marketing

Most marketers for teams have the challenge of filling venues for the rest of the year when the team is not playing. There are also places that have one high profile event per year such as a golf course that hosts a PGA event. The challenge is not just finding new events but also a new set of sponsors and advertisers. Other considerations include government regulations, noise concerns during concerts, and parking considerations. If each event is a one-off, then the resources required to put on the event may not be worth the effort. The concept requires a strategy and then planning for the logistics, and how to market to attendees. Event marketing, more than most marketing stratagems, requires metrics. Some might include:

- Attendance and return to next event
- Social mentions pre and post
- Return on investment
- Partnerships and sponsorships.

Class activity: Have the class, in groups, plan an event to spur tourism that takes place in a large stadium. The class will have fun creating an event. Then ask them to decide if they will price the event at cost plus 10% or cost plus 50%.

Some in the class will say 10% because they want to keep the prices lower. But they will have designed a marvelous event that will have sold out in a stadium with finite seats. Ask them if there is a chance that they might overrun their costs too. The class will see that it is hard to have only 10% above costs. Ask them how they plan to market the event.

Women's Sports

Women's sports have exploded in popularity both in the United States and abroad in the past four years. Women's soccer attracts sellout crowds across Europe, the star-driven WNBA is filling arenas in North America, and athletes like Coco Gauff and Sha'Carri Richardson have global followings. According to DeLoitte Consulting, In 2025, global revenues for women's sports were expected to exceed $2.35 billion dollars (Haskel et al., 2025).

Deloitte's forecast is based on the three main categories of revenue for women's sports; matchday, broadcast and commercial. Commercial revenue, which includes club sponsorships, partnerships, and merchandising sales, currently represents 54 percent of total revenue, followed by broadcast (25 percent) and matchday sales (21 percent).

All 12 WNBA teams in 2024 saw increases in attendance with 154 games as sellouts, more than tripling the number from the previous year. Much is fueled by the stars in the league and the media coverage.

A great interview for the class to watch is David Rubenstein of Peer to Peer on Bloomberg interviewing Cathy Engelbert of the WNBA:

https://www.youtube.com/watch?v=1z7qdP3BW2g

Class activity: In groups, students discuss the pros and cons of women's football or sumo wrestling leagues.

Global Sports

The NFL has played games in London since 2007. NASCAR races in Mexico. The NBA has a strong international base, and you are as likely to see someone in the interior of China wearing a Manchester United sweatshirt as in England. Major League Baseball is especially popular in Japan.

Technology has revolutionized the fan experience. With augmented and virtual reality, fans in some loyalty programs can "be" in the stadium watching their favorite team. Worldwide TV deals let us follow our favorite teams in Indian cricket, the English Premier League, European football, South African rugby and more. Team marketers may use Instagram to share content to engage fans. Platforms such as ESPN+ provide extensive coverage worldwide.

An example of a club with an international following is Real Madrid, which has 2,500 official fan clubs that organize community activities across the globe. Most major soccer clubs now have offices in New York, China, and elsewhere.

A darker side of global sport is sportswashing, when a company or nation uses sport to draw attention away from issues such as human-rights abuses, environmental pollution, or government corruption. Early research suggests that sportswashing can work to change perceptions of host countries. A survey of German viewers found that Qatar's labor difficulties were not improved by its hosting the World Cup, but the Germans had a more-sympathetic attitude toward Arab nations generally (Gläßel, Scharpf, & Edwards, 2025).

Class activity: In groups, organize a fan club for an international sporting club or league outside of the United States. What does the local fan club do and how does it recruit members? How does the club's home country affect perceptions of the team?

Potential Capstones

Here are some choices to give the students as capstone projects:

1 Create a new sports concept to launch in a major city that does not currently exist in that city. Create a comprehensive plan for the launch, including how to get fans and sponsors.

2 Develop a full branding program for a mid-level athlete including social, public relations, community profile, monetary reward.

3 Plan a global launch of merchandise including 4 Ps and analysis and return on investment.

4 Rebrand a team and stadium and all the marketing materials and rebuild the relationship with the fans.

5 Create a sports marketing strategy for the future for a brand. As a teacher, you select the brand which could be Nike, Kind Bars, AT&T, Verizon, Doritos, etc.

Conclusion

Sports marketing positions are in demand for many reasons:

- Strong recognition of the need to use data to reinforce acquisition and retention of consumers and clients

- The rise of global sports
- The need for earned media employing storytelling skills
- New forms of sports and business innovation will grow
- New technologies will be valuable including new ways to use social media
- Sponsorship and partnerships will generate more value
- Skills in communication and creativity in all forms create success.

Jobs range from event planning to fill the stadium in the dormant sports months to analysis of subscriber sales in order to segment communications in the future. If students can provide value for fans to monetize the sports product, if they can utilize technology or data to amplify the sport's value, or if they can innovate or create communications that bring new reasons to give meaning to that sport's product, then the students will likely have jobs.

References

Gläßel, C., Scharpf, A., & Edwards, P. (2025). Does sportswashing work? First insights from the 2022 World Cup in Qatar. *The Journal of Politics, 87*(1). https://www.journals.uchicago.edu/doi/pdf/10.1086/730728

Goi, C. L. (2009). A review of marketing mix: 4Ps or more. *International Journal of Marketing Studies, 1*(1), 2–15. https://pdfs.semanticscholar.org/006a/f4780f1cff9f7075ab5b7073f4cebb32c3d5.pdf/1000

Lawlor, K. B., & Hornyak, M. J. (2012). Smart goals: How the application of smart goals can contribute to achievement of student learning outcomes. *Developments in Business Simulation and Experiential Learning 39*, 259–267. https://journals.tdl.org/absel/index.php/absel/article/view/90/86

Haskel, J; Giogio, P.; Burton, Z., & Tantam, L. (March 17, 2025). Beyond the billion-dollar barrier: Charting the next phase of growth. Deloitte UK. https://www.deloitte.com/content/dam/assets-shared/docs/industries/technology-media-telecommunications/2025/deloitte-womens-sports-2025-v5.pdf

7 Personal Branding in Sports Communication Education

Cara Hawkins-Jedlicka,
Washington State University

Many students aim to become Social Media Influencers (SMI), but collegiate athletes occupy a unique role, balancing competition, academics, and now personal branding as part of their careers. Despite heavy content consumption, many students struggle to build a personal brand that reflects their goals. This highlights the need for personal branding education, especially at the undergraduate level where students face identity development and career pressures.

The need grew after the National Collegiate Athletic Association's (NCAA) Name, Image, and Likeness (NIL) policy took effect on July 1, 2021, opening new revenue opportunities for over 500,000 athletes by allowing them to endorse products and pursue sponsorship deals (Jessop & Sabin, 2021). Since then, sports departments have worked to support athletes adjusting to new roles as entrepreneurs, content creators, and brand ambassadors. As a public relations professor and a former collegiate athlete, I saw an opportunity to provide tools that help collegiate athletes and soon-to-be sports professionals build strategic personal brands. These tools are also valuable for students preparing for careers in digital sports marketing.

Personal branding centers on strategically marketing yourself to others (Brooks & Anumudu, 2016; Gehl, 2011). Students already engage in branding behaviors through clothing choices, social media presence, and daily interactions but often lack the framework to understand these choices (Schau & Gilly, 2003). This course guides students through exercises to identify their core values, strengths, and aspirations, while introducing public relations and marketing principles that explain the connection between their everyday choices and personal branding (Lair et al., 2005; London et al., 2023; Oshiro et al., 2021).

Upon completing the course, students develop key skills in audience analysis, positioning, and content strategy while strengthening their connection to their own identities. The work they produce forms both a foundation for their personal brand and a clear application of branding theory (Scovel, 2023). This course is designed not only for collegiate athletes but also for aspiring sports professionals and sports journalists. It fills a critical gap in personal branding education by equipping students with transferable skills essential for success in the post-NIL collegiate sports world and the broader sports industry job market.

This sixteen-week course is anchored by an every other week in-class discussion. Learning activities fall into four categories: discussions, lectures, content creation, and their own brand plan.

Building Meaning Together: Discussions

The course replaces a traditional textbook with seven discussion-based lessons. Students prepare by reading one of three assigned texts and posting questions to a discussion board. In class, they engage in structured, student-led small group discussions, followed by whole-class sharing to collaboratively build knowledge—a process that fosters "co-meaning" (Hadjioannou, 2007; Parker, 1996). Complementing these discussions, core lectures provide a structured foundation by introducing key concepts.

Teaching the Brand Within: Core Lecture Topics

This course lays the foundation for personal branding through seven core lectures, each offering a broad overview of key topics that could merit a full semester on their own. Together, they help students develop their brand and confidently navigate opportunities.

The History of Personal Branding from Celebrity to Influencers

Self-branding involves strategically crafting a public persona to generate capital (Hearn, 2008). Social media has expanded this practice by enabling content sharing and direct audience engagement, making self-branding more accessible and widespread (Duffy & Pooley, 2019; Kim & McDonald-Liu, 2023). This module examines the evolution of celebrity culture, exploring how Social Media Influencers (SMIs) differ from traditional fame paths. By removing gatekeepers like media outlets and endorsements, social media gives individuals greater control over their narratives and self-presentation (Li et al., 2017). Reflecting this shift, the lecture notes that top-sponsored collegiate athletes often resemble influencers more than professional athletes (Hawkins-Jedlicka & Hall, 2025).

The lesson then explores the fundamentals and evolution of NIL. While NIL rights have long existed, the NCAA formally recognized them in July 2021. The lecture challenges misconceptions such as the idea that all athletes earn millions and highlights the NCAA's historical revenue dependence on unpaid athletes. It also offers a brief history of the NCAA, concluding with ethical issues like the double bind for women athletes, gender inequities, and implications of Title IX (NCAA, n.d.). With this foundation, students begin applying these concepts to themselves, starting with the core question: What makes a brand?

The Basics of Branding and Digital Presence

This lesson introduces branding fundamentals, tracing its evolution and applications in organizations, distinguishing personal from corporate branding, and presenting a brand formula before moving into the planning process (Arora, 2023; Gadiel, n.d.; Wichman et al., 2022). Athlete branding, while related to SMI branding, is shaped by fan awareness, athletic performance, and differentiation from competitors (Montoya, 2002; Hasaan et al., 2018). The Model of Athlete Brand Image (MABI) identifies ten associations across three key dimensions: performance, appearance, and lifestyle (Arai et al., 2013; Yu, 2005). Fans often connect with athletes based on both career success and personal relatability, highlighting branding as a relationship-driven concept (Kunkel et al., 2020a; Escalas & Bettman, 2017; Geurin-Eagleman & Burch, 2016).

Athletes' narratives are often shaped in real time through a combination of media coverage and personal social media use (Scovel, 2024). This lesson introduces framing and media framing theory, which examines how individuals and media construct meaning through selective language and emphasis. Framing theory explains how people interpret or reframe their understanding of an issue (Chong & Druckman, 2007), while media framing theory focuses on how news outlets shape public perception through narrative choices (Borah, 2011; Wilcox & Reber, 2016, p. 24). Often overlooked is the role of framing in public relations, where it is used deliberately to influence how clients and situations are perceived (Hallahan, 1999). This lesson emphasizes that personal branding empowers individuals to frame their own identities rather than being shaped solely by external narratives.

To reinforce this concept, students examine a case study on Hanna and Haley Cavinder, former college basketball players and social media influencers known for their NIL deals. Divided into three groups, students analyze Strauss's (2023) "The NCAA Has a 'Hot Girl' Problem," Carmichael's (2023) "How the Cavinder Twins Blew Up the Student-Athlete Playbook," and the twins' social media profiles. These sources present contrasting frames; one emphasizing sexualization and the other highlighting strategic entrepreneurship. Students contribute descriptive language from their assigned source to a shared board, sparking discussion about media framing, harmful stereotypes, and the role of social platforms, including the twins' public response to Strauss (Cavinder, 2023). Once students can articulate what their brand is, the lesson shifts focus to understanding their audience because without an audience, a personal brand has no impact.

Race, Gender, Sexuality, Identity and Branding

Athletes' personal brands are shaped by their affiliations with teams, sponsors, and governing bodies, as well as by their individual identities, highlighting the intersectionality of branding in sports (Cobbs et al., 2015; Williams et al., 2015). In both collegiate and professional settings, leagues and conferences act as master brands, teams function as sub-brands, and athletes contribute to the overall brand portfolio, influencing perception at every level (Kunkel, Funk, & King, 2014; Williams et al., 2015). These relationships are interconnected; an athlete's association with a team can either enhance or diminish the image of both the team and the larger organization (Balachander & Ghose, 2003; Stevens & Rosenberger, 2012; Kunkel, Funk, & Lock, 2017).

Beyond team affiliation, an athlete's personal brand is also shaped by their sport, cultural expectations, and intersecting identities such as race, gender, class, and ability (Crenshaw, 1991; Duffy & Hund, 2015; Jones et al., 2012). For example, LSU's Flau'jae Johnson, a basketball player and rapper, navigates a different branding landscape than Texas quarterback Arch Manning, whose identity is influenced by a well-known family legacy. These contrasting contexts require distinct branding strategies and reinforce the need to consider intersectionality in personal branding (Uduehi et al., 2024). When audiences are viewed as engaged communities rather than passive spectators, athletes are better positioned to build meaningful connections and foster strong partnerships with teams, leagues, and sponsors (James, 2024; Vardeman-Winter et al., 2013; Shapiro et al., 2017).

Working with Other Brands and Sponsors

One of the most common questions is, "How do I secure sponsorship?" This lesson demystifies the process by examining what audiences and brands seek in partnerships. Athletic sponsorship relies on association; companies aim to transfer athletes' positive public image to their brands, while athletes' unique personalities foster strong connections (Carlson & Donavan, 2013). Social identity theory explains why audiences gravitate toward athlete-endorsed products, as these purchases help express and shape personal identity (Tajfel & Turner, 1985; Carlson & Donavan, 2013).

The lesson then moves beyond basics to focus on achieving specific goals within a broader strategy. Using the G.O.S.T. planning model (Goals, Objectives, Strategies, and Tactics), students learn to develop communication plans that require coordinated efforts rather than isolated actions (Ekka, 2024). It also covers the PESO media model (Paid, Earned, Shared, Owned) and emphasizes the importance of strategic overlap to effectively reach target audiences (Dietrich, 2025). A guest speaker such as a lawyer or agent may join to guide students through basic contract elements, highlighting key points and potential red flags. With a foundation in strategic planning and contract basics, students become better prepared to handle challenges when their brand faces controversy.

Handling Controversy

Collegiate athlete scandals have become more visible and varied, including hazing at Northwestern to sports betting violations at Iowa. Research shows that athletes must actively manage their personal brands, as misconduct can severely damage brand value (Arai et al., 2013; Fink et al., 2009). Students recognize that serious incidents involving athletes, such as Alabama's Brandon

Miller allegedly bringing a gun to a teammate which led to a murder, can trigger national outrage and widespread backlash (Snyder, 2025). However, they often find it harder to recognize the risks of lower-profile issues such as recruitment violations, social media errors, or NIL-related mistakes, all of which can harm reputation. For collegiate athletes, the margin for error is small; even minor mistakes can jeopardize brand deals, playing time, scholarships, and prospects.

This unit introduces image restoration theory through practical case studies. Students first assess anonymized examples to determine if two key assumptions apply: that the accused is responsible for the act and that the act is offensive. In small groups, they develop repair strategies by choosing among five approaches: denial, evasion of responsibility, reducing offensiveness, corrective action, and mortification (Benoit, 2008). Afterward, the real outcomes are revealed for comparison. This lesson deepens students' grasp of image restoration theory and equips them with practical skills to respond to reputational crises.

Branding and Athlete Activism

Activism is increasingly tied to personal branding, as audiences expect public figures to support social causes (Kunkel et al., 2020b). Athlete activism, using one's platform to promote change, can boost fan loyalty and drive social impact (Schmidt et al., 2018). Yet it may also alienate some audiences and harm brand value when seen as controversial (Brown et al., 2022; Frederick et al., 2017; Platt, 2018; Sanderson et al., 2016). Athletes must navigate institutional pressures, team culture, and coaching expectations, so it is crucial to align activism strategically with audience perceptions and personal brand goals (Brown et al., 2022).

NIL is a direct result of collegiate athlete activism. Black collegiate athletes used legal and legislative channels to push for systemic reforms to NCAA policies that included NIL rights and scholarship protections (Crooks et al., 2022). Most collegiate athletes hold favorable views of activism, but engagement remains low due to institutional barriers and potential backlash (Intosh et al., 2020). Due to this, current collegiate athlete activism is more embedded into their daily lives through mentorship and personal storytelling over overt demonstrations (Kluch, 2020). The lesson also explores storytelling beyond sports media by showing how athletes can leverage their brands to raise awareness, with examples like the USWNT's fight for equal pay and the WNBA's role in Black

Lives Matter (Cooky & Antunovic, 2020). The next lesson builds on this by focusing on translating values into a consistent personal brand.

Building a Likeable Brand

This lesson ties everything together by focusing on building a truly likable brand. Students review key concepts and learn to organize messaging using content buckets, which are clear, strategic categories that ensure consistency (Flemming, 2022). By analyzing successful brands and public figures, they explore how curated content shapes perception and builds audience connection. The final lesson challenges students to apply their knowledge, from media framing to activism, in crafting a sustainable personal brand.

Create with Purpose—Content Creation

In this course, students actively develop their personal brands by creating content that highlights their strengths while building communication skills. These hands-on projects equip them to connect with audiences effectively across various platforms. To put their skills into practice, students complete a series of content-driven assignments that integrate strategy, creativity, and personal branding goals:

- **Review Video:** Students create platform-specific video reviews aligned with their brand, gaining camera confidence while leveraging video's growing engagement potential (DeGuzman, 2024).
- **Personal Brand Website:** Students develop websites as central hubs for their personal brands, complete with brand statements and social media integration, establishing control over their digital presence (Jacobson, 2020).
- **Media Kit:** Students design 3–4 page professional media kits highlighting their value, audience, and content capabilities, positioning themselves for potential brand partnerships and sponsorships (Kuzmeski, 2025).

Shaping Your Brand—Plan and Practice

This series of interconnected assignments progressively develops the student's personal brand. By the end of the semester, they will have crafted an actionable personal brand plan ready for implementation. The following assignments support this process:

- **Personal Brand Audit**: Students conduct an audit of their recent social media activity, establishing baseline awareness of their digital presence and current personal brand perception (Brooks & Anumudu, 2016; McCorkle and McCorkle, 2012).
- **Personal Brand Mood Board:** Students translate their brand vision into visual elements through design tools, creating cohesive aesthetic representations that capture their style (Canva, n.d.).
- **Personal Brand Guidelines + Audience Profile:** Through audience research and formal documentation, students define their target demographic while establishing consistent standards for their brand voice, messaging, and visual identity.
- **Personal Brand Strategy**: As a culminating assignment, students develop actionable communication plans with strategies to achieve their personal branding objectives and differentiate themselves (Shafiee et al., 2020).

Conclusion

Effective personal branding goes beyond highlight reels and endorsements. It's about building a community, expressing identity, and communicating one's value in a competitive landscape. Beginning with a personal brand audit, the course helps students develop comprehensive strategies that reflect who they are both on and off the field.

With NIL expanding collegiate athletes' roles as social media influencers, this course highlights a key difference: It's not about the media's portrayal of influencing but intentional, strategic self-presentation. Students learn to engage online with purpose, applying principles from public relations, marketing, and media theory to shape their personal brands.

As NIL continues to transform collegiate athletics, athletes and aspiring sports professionals need skills to balance industry demands with authenticity. This course equips them to do just that. Whether pursuing professional sports, communication careers, or simply sharing their story, students complete the course with a stronger sense of identity and the confidence to tell their own story.

References

Arai, A., Ko, Y.J., & Kaplamidou, K. (2013). Athlete brand image: Scale development and model test. *European Sport Management Quarterly*, *13*(4), 383–403. https://doi.org/10.1080/16184742.2013.811609

Arora, G. (2023, November 12). *What is a brand platform? 14 key components*. Brandfolder. https://brandfolder.com/resources/brand-platform/

Balachander, S., & Ghose, S. (2003). Reciprocal spillover effects: A strategic benefit of brand extensions. *Journal of Marketing*, *67*(1), 4–13.

Benoit, W. L. (2008). Image restoration theory. *The international encyclopedia of communication*.

Borah, P. (2011). Conceptual issues in framing theory: A systematic examination of a decade's literature. *Journal of Communication*, *61*(2), 246–263.

Brooks, A. K., & Anumudu, C. (2016, February). Identity development in personal branding instruction. *Adult Learning*, *27*(1) 23–29. doi: 10.1177/1045159515616968

Brown, S. M., Brison, N. T., Bennett, G., & Brown, K. M. (2022). Do fans care about the activist athlete? A closer look at athlete activism effect on Brand Image. *International Journal of Sport Communication*, *15*(4), 336–344. https://doi.org/10.1123/ijsc.2022-0101

Carlson, B. D., & Donavan, D. T. (2013). Human brands in sport: Athlete brand personality and identification. *Journal of Sport Management*, *27*(3), 193–206. https://doi.org/10.1123/jsm.27.3.193

Carmichael, E. (2023, September 5). How the Cavinder twins blew up the student-athlete playbook. *GQ*. https://www.gq.com/story/cavinder-twins-profile

Canva. (n.d.). *How to build your brand with a Mood Board*. How to build your brand with a mood board. https://www.canva.com/learn/build-brand-mood-board/

Cavinder, H [@CavinderHanna]. (2023, June 13). [Two Images Attached] [Post]. X. https://x.com/CavinderHanna/status/1668754862195212288

Chong, D., & Druckman, J. N. (2007). Framing theory. *Annu. Rev. Polit. Sci.*, *10*(1), 103–126.

Cobbs, Groza, & Rich (2015). Brand spillover effects within a sponsor portfolio: The interaction of image congruence and portfolio size. *Marketing Management Journal*, 25(2), 107–122.

Cooky, C., & Antunovic, D. (2020). "This isn't just about us:" Articulations of feminism in media narratives of athlete activism. *Communication & Sport*, *8*(4–5), 692–711. https://doi.org/10.1177/2167479519896360

Crenshaw, K. (1991). Mapping the margins: Intersectionality, identity politics, and violence against women of color. *Stanford Law Review*, *43*(6), 1241. https://doi.org/10.2307/1229039

Crooks, D., Logan, A., Thomas, D., Clark, L., & Gill, E. (2022). Legal and political activism: The next wave of student-athlete protest. *Sport, Education and Society*, *28*(4), 434–447. https://doi.org/10.1080/13573322.2021.2023490

DeGuzman, D. (2024, December 27). The power of video in news media: How increased audience engagement drives success. *The Associated Press*. https://www.ap.org/insights/the-power-of-video-in-news-media-how-increased-audience-engagement-drives-success/

Dietrich, G. (2025, March 9). A PESO model© primer for marketers and communicators. *Spin Sucks*. https://spinsucks.com/communication/pr-pros-must-embrace-the-peso-model/

Duffy, B. E., & Hund, E. (2015). "Having it all" on social media: Entrepreneurial femininity and self-branding among fashion bloggers. *Social Media + Society*, *1*(2). https://doi.org/10.1177/2056305115604337

Duffy, B. E., & Pooley, J. (2019). Idols of promotion: The triumph of self-branding in an age of precarity. *Journal of Communication*, *69*(1), 26–48. https://doi.org/10.1093/joc/jqy063

Ekka, S. (2024, December 18). GOST model: Goals, objectives, strategies & tactics. Peoplebox. https://www.peoplebox.ai/blog/gost-model/

Escalas, J. E., & Bettman, J. R. (2017). Connecting with celebrities: How consumers appropriate celebrity meanings for a sense of belonging. *Journal of Advertising*, *46*(2), 297–308.

Fleming, B. (2022, June 3). The fool-proof content marketing formula. Brianne Fleming—Brand & Content Marketing with a Pop Culture Twist. https://briannefleming.com/fool-proof-content-marketing-formula/

Frederick, E. L., Sanderson, J., & Schlereth, N. (2017). Kick these kids off the team and take away their scholarships: Facebook and perceptions of athlete activism at the University of Missouri. *Journal of Issues in Intercollegiate Athletics, 10*, 17–34

Fink, J. S., Parker, H. M., Brett, M., & Higgins, J. (2009). Off-field behavior of athletes and team identification: Using social identity theory and balance theory to explain fan reactions. *Journal of Sport Management*, *23*(2), 142–155. https://doi.org/10.1123/jsm.23.2.142

Gadiel, R. (n.d.). Branding in the Digital Age [online workshop], Online. https://generalassemb.ly/education/branding-in-the-digital-age

Gehl, R. W. (2011). Ladders, samurai and blue collars: Personal branding in Web 2.0. *First Monday*, *16*(9) 3–24.

Geurin-Eagleman, A. N., & Burch, L. M. (2016). Communicating via photographs: A gendered analysis of Olympic athletes' visual self-presentation on Instagram. *Sport Management Review*, *19*(2), 133–145.

Hadjioannou, X. (2007). Bringing the background to the foreground: What do classroom environments that support authentic discussions look like? *American Educational Research Journal*, *44*(2), 370–399. https://doi.org/10.3102/0002831207302173

Hallahan, K. (1999). Seven models of framing: Implications for public relations. *Journal of Public Relations Research, 11*(3), 205–242. https://doi.org/10.1207/s1532 754xjprr1103_02

Hasaan, A., Kerem, K., Biscaia, R., & Agyemang, K. (2018). A conceptual framework to understand the creation of athlete brand and its consequences. *International Journal of Sports Marketing and Management, 18*(3), 169–198.

Hawkins-Jedlicka, C. E., & Hall, A. E. (2025). Putting the Image in NIL: How Women's Collegiate Basketball Players Build Personal Brands. In P. J. Creedon & L. A. Wackwitz (Eds.), *Media, Women, and the Transformation of Sport* (pp. 41–63). Routledge.

Hearn, A. (2008, July). Meat, masks, burden: Probing the contours of the branded self. *Journal of Consumer Culture, 8*(2). 197–217. DOI 10.1177/1469540508090086

Intosh, A. M., Martin, E. M., & Kluch, Y. (2020). To act or not to act? Student-athlete perceptions of social justice activism. *Psychology of Sport and Exercise, 51*, 101766. https://doi.org/10.1016/j.psychsport.2020.101766

Jacobson, J. (2020). You are a brand: Social Media Managers' personal branding and "the future audience." *Journal of Product & Brand Management, 29*(6), 715–727. https://doi.org/10.1108/jpbm-03-2019-2299

James, S. (2024). Marketing and communications: An intersectional approach. D&A | Diversity and Ability. https://www.diversityandability.com/marketing-to-an-int ersectional-audience/

Jessop, A., & Sabin, J. (2021). The sky is not falling: Why Name, Image, And Likeness legislation does not violate Title IX and could narrow the publicity gap between men's sport and women's sport athletes. Journal of Legal Aspects of Sport, *31*(2), 253–288.

Jones, S. R., Kim, Y. C., & Skendall, K. C. (2012). (re-) framing authenticity: Considering multiple social identities using autoethnographic and intersectional approaches. *The Journal of Higher Education, 83*(5), 698–724. https://doi.org/10.1080/00221 546.2012.11777263

Kim, E., & McDonald-Liu, C. (2023). Influencers with #NoFilter: How micro-celebrities use self-branding practices on Instagram. *Computers in Human Behavior, 148* 107892, 1–8. https://doi.org/10.1016/j.chb.2023.107892

Kluch, Y. (2020). "My story is my activism!" (Re-)definitions of social justice activism among collegiate athlete activists. *Communication & Sport, 8*(4–5), 566–590. https://doi.org/10.1177/2167479519897288

Kunkel, T., Funk, D. C., & King, C. (2014). Developing a conceptual understanding of consumer-based league brand associations. *Journal of Sport Management, 28*(1), 49–67.

Kunkel, T., Funk, D. C., & Lock, D. (2017). The effect of league brand on the relationship between the team brand and behavioral Intentions: A formative approach examining brand associations and brand relationships. *Journal of Sport Management*, *31*(4), 317–332.

Kunkel, T., Biscaia, R., Arai, A., & Agyemang, K. (2020a). The role of self-brand connection on the relationship between athlete brand image and Fan Outcomes. *Journal of Sport Management*, *34*(3), 201–216. https://doi.org/10.1123/jsm.2019-0222

Kunkel, T., Doyle, J., & Na, S. (2020b). Becoming more than an athlete: Developing an athlete's personal brand using strategic philanthropy. *European Sport Management Quarterly*, *22*(3), 358–378. https://doi.org/10.1080/16184 742.2020.1791208

Kuzmeski, M. (2025). *Name, Image & Likeness: Personal Branding Strategies for Student-athletes*. Stukent. 2025, https://www.stukent.com/higher-ed/name-image-likeness/

Lair, D. J., Sullivan, K., & Cheney, G. (2005). Marketization and the recasting of the professional self. *Management Communication Quarterly*, *18*(3), 307–343. https://doi.org/10.1177/0893318904270744

Li, B., Stokowski, S., Dittmore, S. W., Malmo, J. R., & Rolfe, D. T. (2017). A case study of self-representation on Twitter: A gender analysis of how student-athletes portray themselves. *Global Sport Business Journal*, *5*(1), 61–75.

London, M., Sessa, V. I., & Shelley, L. A. (2023). Developing self-awareness: Learning processes for self- and interpersonal growth. *Annual Review of Organizational Psychology and Organizational Behavior*, *10*(1), 261–288. https://doi.org/10.1146/annurev-orgpsych-120920-044531

McCorkle, D.E. & McCorkle, Y. L. (2012, Summer). Using LinkedIn in the marketing classroom: Exploratory insights and recommendations for teaching social networking. *Marketing Education Review*, *22*(2) 157–166.

Montoya, P. (2002). *The Personal Branding Phenomenon*. Nashville, TN: Personal Branding Press.

NCAA. (n.d.). *History*. NCAA.org. https://www.ncaa.org/sports/2021/5/4/hist ory.aspx

Parker, W. C. (1996). Curriculum for democracy. *Democracy, education, and the schools*, 182–210.

Platt, L. (2018). Athlete activism is on the rise, but so is the backlash. *Global Sports Matters*. https://globalsportmatters.com/culture/2018/ 04/16/athlete-activism-is-on-the-rise-but-so-is-the-backlash/

Oshiro, K. F., Brison, N., & Bennett, G. (2021). Personal branding project in a sport marketing class. *Journal of Hospitality, Leisure, Sport &; Tourism Education*, *28*, 100308. https://doi.org/10.1016/j.jhlste.2021.100308

Sanderson, J., Frederick, E., & Stocz, M. (2016). When athlete activism clashes with group values: Social identity threat management via social media. *Mass Communication and Society*, *19*(3), 301–322.

Scovel, S. (2023). *JOUR-459W: Sports media & athlete branding* [Syllabus]. The Philip Merrill College of Journalism, University of Maryland.

Scovel, S. (2024). Mentioned, quoted, and promoted: How sports journalists constructed a narrative of athletes' value in the "name, image, and likeness" ERA. *International Journal of Sport Communication, 17*(4), 417–430. https://doi.org/10.1123/ijsc.2024-0063

Schau, H. J. & Gilly, M. C. (2003, December). We are what we post? Self-presentation in personal web space. *Journal of Consumer Research, 30*(3) 385–404.

Schmidt, S. H., Shreffler, M. B., Hambrick, M. E., & Gordon, B. S. (2018). An experimental examination of activist type and effort on brand image and purchase intentions. *Sports Marketing Quarterly, 27*(1), 31–43. https://doi.org/10.32731/SMQ.271.032018.03

Shafiee, M., Gheidi, S., Khorrami, M. S., & Asadullah, H. (2020). Proposing a new framework for personal brand positioning. *European Research on Management and Business Economics, 26*, 45–54. https://doi.org/10.1016/j.iedeen.2019.12.002

Shapiro, S. L., DeSchriver, T. D., & Rascher, D. A. (2017). The Beckham effect: Examining the longitudinal impact of a star performer on league marketing, novelty, and scarcity. *European Sport Management Quarterly, 17*(5), 610–634.

Snyder, A. (2025, May 9). Former Alabama standout, NBA star Brandon Miller testifies in Michael Lynn Davis capital murder trial. *The Tuscaloosa News*. https://www.tuscaloosanews.com/story/sports/college/basketball/2025/05/08/nba-star-brandon-miller-testifies-in-michael-lynn-davis-capital-murder-trial-alabama-basketball/83516229007/

Strauss, E. (2023, June 13). The NCAA has a 'hot girl' problem. *The Free Press*. https://www.thefp.com/p/the-ncaa-and-the-cavender-twins

Stevens, S., & Rosenberger, P. J. (2012). The influence of fan involvement, following sport and fan identification on fan loyalty: An Australian perspective. *International Journal of Sports Marketing & Sponsorship*, 13(3), 220–234.

Tajfel, H., & Turner, J. C. (1985). *The social identity theory of intergroup behavior.* Nelson-Hall.

Uduehi, E., Saint Clair, J. K., & Crabbe, R. (2024). Intersectionality in marketing: A paradigm for understanding understudied consumers. *Journal of Marketing*. https://doi.org/10.1177/00222429241258493

Vardeman-Winter, J., Tindall, N., & Jiang, H. (2013). Intersectionality and publics: How exploring publics' multiple identities questions basic public relations concepts. *Public Relations Inquiry, 2*(3), 279–304. https://doi.org/10.1177/2046147x13491564

Wichmann, J. R., Wiegand, N., & Reinartz, W. J. (2022). Building your own brand platform. *Harvard Business Review, 100*(5), 47–53.

Wilcox, D. L., & Reber, B. H. (2016). *Public relations writing and media techniques* (8th ed.). Pearson.

Williams, A., Kim, D. Y., Agyemang, K., & Martin, T. G. (2015). All brands are not created equal: Understanding the role of athletes in sport-brand architecture. *Journal of Multidisciplinary Research, 7*(3), 75–86.

Yu, C. (2005). Athlete endorsement in the international sport industry: A case study of David 1093 Beckham. *International Journal of Sports Marketing and Sponsorship, 6*(3), 189–99.

8 Advice for Teaching Esports

Kacey Doran, Rowan University

Teaching esports is a lot of fun and an important, developing part of the competitive entertainment scene. In this chapter, I'll share my cheat codes[1] for how to get started teaching esports at your school. I'll give a brief explanation of esports themselves, some tips for hiring esports professors, outline some suggestions for organizing curriculum, highlight some types of classes for the programs, and unpack some classroom content.

What Are Esports?

Esports are video game competitions involving matches where at least two human players compete against one another. A game can be one person versus another, like the fighting game Mortal Kombat, or esports teams can be formed by creating a group of at least three players. While many players can make money through streaming games for revenue and/or signing with sponsors, players on esports teams can also earn money like traditional sports athletes. To earn money like traditional sports athletes, esports teams enter circuits where the matches often start in a virtual format, then move to an in-person format in the semi-final and final matches, complete with a live audience. In the higher levels in the most popular games, esports players can sign contracts; some are even salaried. The media coverage required for the human players as well as the digital playing field makes esports a natural fit for production and communications departments (thus, its home at Rowan University). The professional focus of esports also makes business a logical area of study (like at Drexel University). Other integral elements of the global,

---

[1]Cheat codes are like passwords that players can enter into videogames to make playing easier. For example, it might make the character they're playing stronger, or they might instantly get a lot of in-game currency they can spend to bypass difficult challenges.

organized videogames tournaments open possibilities for esports programs to exist with a focus oncomponents such as event planning, game design, social media, and other applicable fields.

How to Hire Esports Professors

All industries benefit from professors who work in the field and share their experience and expertise in the classroom, and esports are no different. Esports courses tend to fill, especially once the word gets out that students can talk about videogames for credit. The ideal esports professors should bring a variety of industry and teaching experiences, as well as all levels and forms of education. Understanding esports requires so much more than what one person alone can provide, so ensure that you assemble an esports team with individuals who have a wide variety of different experiences and expertise. Professors with different kinds of teaching experience, like coaching as opposed to traditional academic instruction, are encouraged. Experience with keeping students safe and organized in the esports environment, combined with insider information are great starting points for a coach learning to become a teacher. Further, professors with administrative experience or experience with startups can provide tips in the fields of esports management and tournament organization, including methods for fundraising and in-person networking. Esports journalists provide a unique perspective on both the history of esports development and sports coverage overall. Professors with experience using Discord and Twitch are crucial to developing courses in social media, marketing and advertising, and networking online, and can even contribute to student skillsets in online design and video editing.

Part-time Versus Full-time Esports Professors

It can't be stressed enough that esports are incredibly interdisciplinary, which presents exciting possibilities and challenges for hiring full-time professors. Therefore, hiring a full-time professor with experience and expertise in two or more disciplines in a position that spans at least two departments is ideal. Interdisciplinary and/or interdepartmental focuses increase the number of tools at the professor's disposal, give them more opportunities to collaborate with other educators, staff, and administrators across campus, and lend rigor to the esports research by encouraging borrowing from and modifying theories and practices from other disciplines. Full-time professors can also function as esports team managers and coaches. This allows them the structures to help students make connections between their competitive play on teams, their classwork, and internships involved with esports competitions, as well as more casual events.

For the hiring of part-time professors, job ads should focus primarily on esports. Emphasizing experience with analyzing professional competitions as opposed to videogames more broadly helps direct your search. Additionally, industry experience and leniency on educational certification assists with building a part-time pool. Part-time esports professors are often some of the most qualified subject experts. The highest levels of professional esports have different seasons like traditional sports, but these are often short, anywhere from one to two and a half months, making the flexibility of adjunct schedules often ideal for these professors.

Esports courses are often taught online, given esports' history of developing and the current popularity of online gaming as well as the desire to make use of free software for video projects often assigned in esports courses. Thus, onboarding is especially important for professors of these online, asynchronous classes. Set clear expectations about how often professors should communicate with students, what level of lateness and Generative AI use by students will be tolerated, and when professors need to submit information such as attendance verification and final grades. Because your professors are likely from a variety of backgrounds, take the time to support and evaluate them based on their needs. Be willing to recommend training in DEI—at schools that provide it—or workshops on engaging teaching methods. We suggest a copy of *Master Class: Teaching Advice for Journalism and Mass Communication Instructors* (Roush, 2017). Be aware that part-time professors often feel disconnected, due to less demands from the institution on their time than the full-time faculty. Thus, make sure all esports professors receive important information.

How to Organize an Esports Curriculum

We want a student seeking a career in esports to be a jack of a few trades. Candidates for esports industry positions are often expected to do a few skilled tasks in their positions. To best support your students, focus on the interdisciplinary nature of the field and create courses that cover the business, production, and other sides of esports. This can look different in practice based on where your program is located and the opportunities available to students. In New Jersey, where Rowan University is housed, and nearby Philadelphia, Pennsylvania, there are steadily increasing entertainment industry opportunities. Philadelphia includes several large stadiums requiring camera operation, commentating, and organizational positions. Esports were recently recognized as part of varsity sports in the New Jersey school system and are also developing as part of STEM and art programs, which will require even more skilled workers in educational, coaching, and management positions. Finally, large media companies are in negotiations or have already set up shop in New Jersey, taking advantage of its proximity to New York and other large cities. Esports students with experience combinations have the ability to organize professional events, comfortably network, advertise, or provide coverage of competitions across social media and live broadcasts, and use their background knowledge on gaming and production technology in commercial, corporate, and academic settings are, and will only become more, invaluable in this tri-state area as well as other entertainment hubs nationally and globally.

Encourage students to double major and take an interdisciplinary approach to their degree. Rowan University's degree is flexible with a selection of concentrations in communications, business, and computing. While you can make your program as rigorous as any other, esports degrees still benefit from being paired with more established disciplines to lend them legitimacy. More importantly, students directing their educational path can motivate class attendance and participation, introduce them to skills and interests that make them uniquely skilled workers, and create novel, cross-disciplinary opportunities.

One of the most important experiences your students will have is internships, even when not exclusively with esports groups. Develop multiple pathways to ensure students will have worthwhile internship opportunities. Some of these include making use of your professors with industry connections, creating partnerships with esports-friendly companies, aligning with school districts to hire your students to organize and run their tournaments, and collaborating with other colleges and universities to compete in, host, and stream competitions.

Partnerships are beneficial to esports programs. They can provide expensive equipment and valuable space for your students' events and competitions. Beware of predatory businesses, which developed after esports soared to popularity during the second half of the 2010s. Make sure to consult multiple sources before signing contracts, including, and especially, your professors, staff, and administration, whom you've vetted and hired from the industry.

Regardless of how you begin your program, don't hesitate to reach out to other departments to incorporate different disciplines. Other departments to consider connecting with your esports programs can range from sociology and making use of qualitative research for esports oral histories to computer science and game development for critical background knowledge of frequently updated and incredibly popular computer-based esports games. Production skills like video editing, streaming management, and podcasting script writing are valuable for esports coverage that will get students noticed in the job market as well as transferable skills in other kinds of online and streaming entertainment. Media literacy through humanities and communications departments like history, American studies, and journalism help students get a better grasp on the media landscape that's influenced esports' development. Lastly, business departments that focus on marketing and funding trends can help students develop tools and tips for avoiding pitfalls by examining the recent esports and crypto financial bubbles that burst at the end of the 2010s and whose effects have continued to ripple into the 2020s.

As the above examples have illustrated, many opportunities exist between business, media, sports, and creative industries and those corresponding areas in your school. Esports jobs are constantly changing due to the nature of the industry, audiences, and the ever-shifting relationship with different kinds of technology. If you see something in your research that looks promising or find a gap in coverage, business, design, or the like, check it out! Consult professors with industry experience, other professors in interrelated fields, as well as chairs, directors, and deans.

Different Types of Courses for Esports Programs

The main goals for esports programs should center around graduates' abilities to understand, analyze, evaluate and apply core concepts within esports and the esports industry. Students should be prepared to achieve practical and professional goals through gaining skills like shoutcasting (the esports equivalent of sports broadcasting), in-game observing (the technique of moving around the virtual videogame field to cover specific plays), and journalistic esports reporting. Students should use sociocultural approaches to understand the continued marginalization of certain groups (for example, women and minorities) by the gatekeepers in gaming communities, as well as esports' global opportunities to create more welcoming competitive spaces. Thus, graduates should be strong communicators, critical thinkers, and ethically driven professionals who can make sound decisions about the implications of their actions. Finally, creating different concentrations for students allows them to demonstrate expertise in a range of areas of study and related disciplines as appropriate to their professional and academic objectives.

In addition to esports being a relatively new field with a history of mostly being online, all college students will need technological skills in their future careers. Incorporating a variety of multimodal and experiential learning opportunities in your curriculum is recommended to allow them to develop these technological skills. For lower stakes assignments, have students make short recordings of the games they're already playing. Assign students a specific concept and have them explain it to the viewer while they're showing it through gameplay. Some assignments include having students show they understand the basics of the esports game, explain how competitive gameplay is different from casual, and share some personal connections.

As students progress through the degree, higher stakes assignments involve multiple parts, event organization, and specific skillsets. In esports reporting, students interview professionals in the esports industry, requiring research, multiple forms of communication, recording, transcribing, writing, and editing stages. Esports internships often involve coordinating esports tournaments including logistics like transportation, providing food, setup and cleanup, and securing funding for prizes. Finally, students can learn more advanced techniques in video editing for social media, documentaries, and so forth, and in-game observing.

There are scholarly sources specifically for esports and useful videogame theories for the kind of analysis expected of your students in the industry. However, esports documentaries are some of the richest primary sources for esports information. The visual depiction of communities, professional tournaments, and the evolution of gaming software and hardware is effective both in the classroom and as an online assignment.

Esports courses should unpack the competitive and team-based nature of esports. One way for assignments to reinforce this is to require that students play against friends and family or randomly selected online opponents rather than computer players (often referred to as CPU's because you're playing against the computer's ability to process gameplay) or single-player games that don't have game modes allowing multiplayer competition. There's no overstating the influence of the internet on esports, and it's therefore required in introductory, technically and historically focused courses. Widespread internet availability starting in the 1990s allowed for multiplayer competition online, which set the stage for early competitions formalized into in-person tournaments with large and/or cash prizes. Further, esports bear similar historical burdens as other media, sports, and videogames: discrimination that needs to be challenged, especially with the proliferation of online spaces. Likewise, South Korean tournaments being supported by large sponsorships starting in the early 2000s and COVID forcing everyone to interact from a distance simultaneously brought more attention to different esports games and their potential. Finally, the global material and cultural differences between countries creates context for why different esports games, leagues, lobbies, and gaming cafes exist as well as which groups favor playing console-based, mobile, or PC games.

Esports Are Always Changing, But Here's What's Not

"Esports" are referred to plurally because they, like traditional sports and other media, encompass different genres of competitive videogames. Moreover, esports are determined as much by the audience as they are by professional players and organizations. If a video game doesn't have an audience, then there isn't the desire or interest to create tournaments and opportunities for watching and engaging with games. Most esports audiences exist online watching through Twitch, YouTube, Discord, and other online streaming platforms. The largest games have been hosted at indoor and outdoor stadiums, featuring other entertainment like live musical performances as takes place during American football games. These in-person audiences don the esports team's uniforms but also wear everything from headpieces to full cosplay[2] of popular videogame characters who are and aren't part of the esports games.

Esports audiences watch and root for their favorite teams and players like traditional sports fans. However, skill acquisition adds an additional component to viewership. Players of the esports games often watch esports

---

[2]Dressing up like characters from videogames, animated shows and films, comic books, anime, and manga. This is a common part of convention culture. It's expected dress as well as sometimes part of events like costume contests.

streamers, ranked[3] players, and/or teams to learn from the best in the hopes of incorporating it into their own play. Traditional sports have established teams associated with cities and countries, existing in physical locations and facing certain limitations. Fans typically stick with 'their' team through thick and thin. Conversely, esports mostly exist online, which makes them more accessible to a broader audience.

Esports games can go in and out of favor among fans and have only more recently in the 2020s received support from publishing companies like Nintendo. Video games with esports scenes, such as Madden football, come out with new versions each year, and online games like League of Legends can be updated, altering the competitive scene overnight. The availability of an online video game to be changed quickly is both a boon and threat to the accessibility of esports. Publishers can cut access to a game by putting it behind a paywall or shut out access to a specific console. Even getting gaming computers powerful enough to run esports games is a hurdle. As a result of this fluctuation, it behooves curriculum coordinators to make the case for frequent updates. Information on the competitive scene quickly goes out of date and updates to coverage techniques are constantly being made. Assignments need to be relevant and allow room for experimentation and practice to prepare students. Multiple drafts and flexibility are recommended and encouraged; students need to see the improvement of their work through editing and to become as comfortable as possible with problem solving personal, academic, gaming, production, and other useful kinds of technology. Leave space in your syllabus whenever possible to take advantage of esports current events.

Some Nitty Gritty[4] Pro Tips

Our students are "subject experts" about esports, says Rutgers-Camden's Dr. Claire Strickland, and one of the most exciting and rewarding parts of teaching esports courses is giving your students the opportunity to teach you. It's unrealistic to expect any film professor to know everything about every movie in a specific genre, and it's the same for an esports professor. Instead,

---

[3]Talented players can ascend and descend ranks for appropriately challenging matches against other players. This keeps players of the same skill battling against each other to make the games more exciting and prevent shutouts that discourage new players.
[4]I am a Pennsylvanian gamer and a Philadelphia sports fan. (Gritty is the Philadelphia Flyers mascot.)

the assignments that are most successful allow students to be excited about their favorite games, then scaffolding their assignments through examples, case studies, and categorization.

Icebreakers are the perfect way to start an in-person course, while introductory posts work better for online courses. Ideally, you learn about your student's major, current career goals, and their favorite video game. Make room for discussions about the sports they enjoy and/or play as well as how their play and free time have changed over time. The more connections that can be made between popular esports, traditional sports and esports' historical growth, and the kind of skills students will need in their desired careers, the more effective your students will be at completing classwork and become empowered to speak and write about games they enjoy and a growing industry that interests them.

Watch out for students making assumptions about what their readers and/or audience know about esports, videogames, and sports. Especially in the introductory, lower level, and elective classes without prerequisites, students must have the ability to explain the basics of the games. This includes explaining terms about the esports games and commonly used terms between esports teammates. Additionally, create check-in assignments before larger assignments involving competitive games. Some students have trouble separating competitive esports against other players from videogames that are more story-driven and meant to be immersive, single-player experiences.

More optimistically, esports offer young people more options to participate in social groups, feel empowered competing for their school or community, and partnerships for school districts, libraries, and other community groups to gain access to necessary technology to support their students, patrons, and residents. Academically, the regular shift of popular esports allows for flexibility in your syllabus. Students can bring in new games and add to the analytic potential of assignments. Esports can break historic trends and current mainstream conceptions of videogames, especially those with fighting and shooting gameplay, and have already made waves through diverse representation in their selection of characters for players to use.

Reference

Roush, C. (2017). *Master class: Teaching advice for journalism and mass communication instructors*. Rowman & Littlefield.

Part III
Finding Partners

9 Getting Students in the Game

Negotiating Real World Experiences in Sports Media Education

Welch Suggs, University of Georgia

Experiential learning has become imperative in many disciplines in higher education, especially as universities seek to demonstrate their ability to prepare students for careers. Media fields—particularly journalism—have a jump on other departments, because experiential learning has been part of the curriculum at most institutions going back to the origins of the Missouri Method, the ethos of the University of Missouri's School of Journalism, which owns media outlets and staffs them with students (Wanta, 2025). Gathering background information, interviewing, and producing stories can be discussed in a classroom environment, but learning these skills and the mindset required to execute them requires students to go out into the "real world" to understand what is needed of them.

The world of sports produces both challenges and opportunities for instructors trying to create experiential opportunities for their students. Unlike other forms of news, sports happens on a schedule, and teams have their own infrastructure to support internal and external media. But many teams attract such high levels of interest from fans and media that students can be crowded out of opportunities for meaningful professional experiences. This chapter lays out the landscape of sports media relations to help instructors work with professionals to create the environment their students need to learn how to produce great stories.

Background: Access as a "Subsidy"

To understand how sports and news organizations work with one another, it can be helpful to look at the broader context of organizations interacting with journalists. After all, journalists have no intrinsic rights or power to be in spaces or require anyone to speak to them. As a result, customs and rituals have evolved in all areas of society governing whether media are welcome. At the federal level, in the nineteenth century, as the press broke free of partisan affiliation and became more impartial, governments granted news organizations certain "subsidies" (Cook, 2012). For example, the U.S. Postal Service offered favorable rates to periodicals, federal agencies established press bureaus, politicians published press releases, and the Senate in 1841 built a special gallery for the press. The goal was to increase press coverage of what the government was doing, and undoubtedly to try to elicit more positive stories, but the routines and expectations of press access have become ingrained in political culture.

As organized sports grew and attracted public attention in the early twentieth century, teams eagerly solicited media coverage by providing reporters with similar kinds of subsidies—free access to prime seats, allowing them to travel on trains, giving them access to locker rooms and interviews, and so forth. This often led to accusations that sportswriters were less ethical than their colleagues elsewhere in the newsroom, giving the sports desk the sobriquet the "Toy Department of the Newspaper" (Hardin, Zhong, & Whiteside, 2009; Rowe, 2007). But the popularity of sports at all levels made the sports pages consistent profit centers for news organizations, forming a symbiotic relationship between sportswriters and the teams they covered.

While that summary leaves a lot to be unpacked, the relevant part for this topic is this: Sports organizations have sets of customs and routines in place to allow journalists to attend games and to interview key personnel at designated times and places. With the cooperation of a given team, these practices can be used to provide a high-quality learning environment for sports media students.

Before getting into specifics of how this works, it's worth noting that these customs and routines differ from one team to another, even within the same sport or the same community. Teams develop their own cultures of dealing with the media, based on the histories and personalities of the professionals involved. So sports-media professors seeking to negotiate opportunities for students cannot take exactly what happens in one set of circumstances and transfer it to another.

Working with Teams and Communications Professionals

High Schools

Generally speaking, Athletic Directors (ADs) at the school or district level are the best starting point in discussing whether the school or district is comfortable having sports-media students cover teams and events. ADs will have some understanding of non-athletic administration policy and culture when it comes to media access, as well as knowledge of coaches and which ones are open to having their teams and games covered. Generally speaking, many coaches and ADs will not object to such coverage unless they perceive it as a stress on their players or if they have too many responsibilities to want to engage with this.

Some schools/districts may require college students to complete a background check and/or undergo training about working with minors to work with high school athletes. This is common in student-teaching environments and is starting to spread to contexts, such as media.

High schools can be great opportunities to cover teams and events because access is relatively easy, and students often enjoy getting the attention of being interviewed by college students. However, coaches may be difficult to contact for interview or coverage requests, and students may be shy talking about themselves. Moreover, reliable statistics and background information—and even schedules—can be hard to come by. Even sites like MaxPreps and Hudl may be outdated or contain inaccuracies, so reporters must be prepared to verify information with coaches or other team staff.

Colleges and Universities

First, some definitional notes. America has more than 2,000 colleges with intercollegiate athletic programs. In 2022–23, athletic programs ranged in size from one athlete to nearly 1,300, according to the U.S. Department of Education's Office of Postsecondary Education. Over half of them belong to the National Collegiate Athletic Association (NCAA), with the others dispersed among the National Association for Intercollegiate Athletics (NAIA), the National Junior College Athletic Association (NJCAA), and other national-level organizations. The NCAA consists of three divisions: In Division III, colleges are required to have 10 to 12 sports (depending on enrollment) and cannot award athletic financial aid. Division II members can award limited financial aid and must sponsor at least ten sports. Division I members offer at least 16 sports and athletic financial aid to most if not all athletes, with higher requirements for members of the Football Bowl Subdivision, that is, colleges whose teams play in postseason bowl games. At the highest level are the Power Four or Autonomy conferences: the Atlantic Coast, Big 12, Big Ten and Southeastern Conferences, whose members comprise the largest flagship and land-grant universities in the country along with a handful of private research universities. Their athletic departments bring in hundreds of millions of dollars in ticket sales, donations, broadcast revenue, and postseason contests in men's basketball and football. Although only a tiny proportion of the college athletics landscape, Power Four institutions suck up virtually all of the media attention devoted to college sports.

Virtually all athletic programs have a communications department that might be called sports information, athletic communications, athletic media relations, or something similar. For decades the main function of these operations was to enable outside media to cover teams by issuing credentials, arranging interviews, maintaining statistics, and creating press releases and media guides. In the twenty-first century, those roles have grown to include creating multimedia content for athletic websites and social-media feeds, staffing over-the-air and digital game broadcasts, and even helping athletes market themselves through the kinds of sponsorship contracts known as Name, Image and Likeness (NIL) deals. (Sometimes these functions are spread among multiple departments, depending on the size and complexity of the athletic program.) The sports communication officer (long known as the sports information director) can be the sole full-time employee performing these roles at many institutions; at Power Four institutions, athletic departments may have 20 or more professionals working full-time in communications roles, along with part-time student workers (paid and unpaid) and graduate assistants. The majority of communications resources will be directed to revenue sports, but every team will have a media contact, a media guide, a web page with press releases and player information, and other basics. This is true no matter what the division or association is in which the athletic program competes.

Despite all the changes in both technology and practice in sports media, the basic process of requesting a credential and/or an interview with players and coaches hasn't changed: You call (or e-mail) the sports communications contact for that team. Sports media professors and students can follow the exact same process to discuss options for covering games or procuring interviews for stories. Policies, of course, will depend on the athletic department in question.

Most sports venues have some form of press seating, but news outlets are sending fewer reporters to cover games. As such there may be room for a class or a specific number of students to attend games and postgame media conferences to gather information for story assignments. Teams also will typically have availabilities scheduled during the weekend when media can interview coaches and athletes. Reporters may need to ask for specific athletes to ensure they attend the availability.

All of this is to say that the structures are in place with hundreds if not thousands of college teams for non-professional media to cover games. Moreover, many coaches, athletes, and media staff recognize the value of providing media access as an educational opportunity. Big-time programs with extensive media demands may not have the time or desire to open themselves up to student media, however, and coaches and athletes in other sports may not want to interrupt postgame routines to conduct interviews.

Professional Sports

In the United States, media access is written into the collective bargaining agreements that professional leagues sign with players, so there are processes for pregame and postgame locker room access established much more formally than at the high school or collegiate level. Whether team media staff will be amenable to allowing students to access those or to cover events depends entirely on the individuals involved. Teams also have designated availabilities around practices and other events, which student media may be able to attend.

Minor league teams in sports such as soccer, hockey and basketball may welcome students if their venues have space to accommodate them. The same goes for major league teams on nights where lower-profile opponents are in town. These experiences can be exhilarating for students being "backstage" at a professional sporting event, but access to coaches and players is generally quite limited.

As minor and semiprofessional leagues proliferate, some organizations will be welcoming to students covering games and conducting interviews. But for many teams, media staff are stretched across creating social media content, generating press releases, assisting with promotions, and even calling games for broadcast or streaming services. Moreover, without media to cover them, newer franchises may not have developed the same routines for access that major league and established franchises have adopted over decades of play. The same may be true for women's professional teams in volleyball, soccer, and other sports. Also, in sports like soccer, international players may not be accustomed to the kind of postgame access that is common in American sports and may not welcome reporters asking questions.

Considerations to Balance

Covering events and interviewing coaches and athletes allows students to build real-world skills in having professional conversations, gathering information, and producing stories on deadline. These are experiences that demonstrate media skills that translate to many career fields. But in designing classroom assignments that require some level of access, instructors need to keep a number of human factors in mind.

First, is the request for access reasonable? Expecting a coach or athlete to drop everything to participate in an interview immediately or even on less than a day's notice usually would not be considered reasonable, nor would walking up to a game and requesting a credential on the spot. As with any kind of interview or professional request in a media space, the more lead time, the better.

Second, how disruptive is the access request? Getting students into a crowded press box would require a lot of work from the communications staff. Similarly, a one-on-one interview request might require more time than a coach or player is willing to give. Another common problem is overwhelming a sports-communication pro with too many requests in too short a time.

Third, did the request follow the right protocol? Students are often tempted to reach out directly to athletes, particularly if those athletes are friends or classmates. But doing so can cause problems with sports communication personnel who are tasked with managing access (and face complaints from professional media who feel undercut by students). Coaches and other staff also do not appreciate direct contact from the media out of the blue.

And fourth, what's in it for the subject? Some sports communications staff and their teams will be willing to provide access merely as an educational opportunity, but if there is some benefit to them, such as publicity, they will be more willing to grant access. Can student work get published in local media outlets, bringing attention to teams and athletes that don't usually get it? Could stories or other forms of content be generated for the athletic department to use on its channels? If students in a class are producing stories for student media, that may be enough of an additional incentive.

Ultimately, if instructors can work with sports-communication personnel far enough in advance to create opportunities for event coverage or prepare students to make their own requests for credentials and interviews, they can put students in enormously beneficial situations to strengthen their abilities. Equally important, though, is structuring assignments to provide feedback on whether students used the opportunity to get the right information and produce professional stories, and what they should have done differently in the moment. Doing so creates a much more meaningful educational experience than merely touring a press box or writing a practice story for homework.

Beyond Access

Sports organizations have become increasingly focused on producing their own media on all platforms—broadcasts and live streams, social content creation, team reporting, and traditional media relations products like press releases and media guides. This is true at all levels of competition, including high schools, youth sports organizations, collegiate clubs, intercollegiate sports at all levels, and professional and semiprofessional/minor league teams, as well as leagues and athletic conferences. Fan engagement and sponsorship activation are also becoming increasingly important to sports organizations. All of these can be valuable opportunities for students to get work experience, whether in a class environment, as internships, or in student worker positions.

How does an instructor or an academic program structure these experiences? Some are fairly natural: Most high school sports happen within the timeframe of an academic semester and high schools lack professional media staff, so students in a social content creation class can adopt local teams as clients for the duration of a season. Collegiate sports programs often hire interns, student workers and graduate assistants for year-long (or multi-year) jobs in sports communication, promotion, marketing, and other areas. Students can work in broadcast production either in a class setting or as contract employees, but it can be difficult to get them ready to work as professionals quickly enough to have a full experience during a semester that might last 14 or 15 weeks. But teams also can build opportunities for students to advance in their capabilities and responsibilities. For example, students may gain entry-level experience working with a local club and parlay that into higher-level tasks with an intercollegiate or professional team.

The key consideration in designing any of these opportunities is whether students receive enough critique and feedback to know if they are executing to a professional standard and how they can improve. Instructors can provide some of this feedback, but the supervisors employing students as interns or contractors are much better positioned to assess the quality of student work, if they are willing to do so. This leads to the question of whether sports organizations pay interns or not: If they are willing to help students grow and develop their skills, there may be circumstances whether an unpaid internship is worth it. But if a small local organization lacking media expertise employs a student, it's hard to justify the value of experience without paying them.

Conclusion

Journalism and other media fields are professionally oriented. As a deputy sports editor from the Associated Press told a group of our students in spring 2025, "If the most interesting thing about your resume is your G.P.A., I don't have anything for you to do." It is incumbent upon students to seek out professional opportunities to demonstrate their skills and to prove their value in the job market through portfolios of work samples and references from industry professionals. It is also incumbent upon instructors to help students build the groundwork for those experiences through in-class experiences and applying for internships and other kinds of positions. This is not to discount the ethics, background knowledge, and history that students also should be learning in class; indeed, one can argue that studying broad-based liberal arts and science fields while getting high quality experiences out of class is better preparation for a media professional than focusing on a narrow major such as sports journalism. But instructors in sports media can benefit tremendously from learning the work routines and workplace expectations of professionals in the field and showing students what to expect "in the real world."

References

Cook, T. E. (2012). *Governing with the news: The news media as a political institution.* University of Chicago Press.

Hardin, M., Zhong, B., & Whiteside, E. (2009). Sports coverage: "Toy department" or public-service journalism? The relationship between reporters' ethics and attitudes toward the profession. *International Journal of Sport Communication, 2*(3), 319–339.

Rowe, D. (2007). Sports journalism: Still the toy department' of the news media? *Journalism, 8*(4), 385–405.

Wanta, W. (2025). Journalism Education in the US—Past, Present, Future. *Media Research Issues, 68*(1), 13–20.

10 Back in the Game
Reviving a Campus Newspaper Through a Sports Writing Course
Nick Hirshon,
William Paterson University

Matt Goldman had a problem: a source who wouldn't open up. He was profiling a member of the bowling team at William Paterson University, a regional public institution in Wayne, New Jersey, 20 miles from New York City. The draft he turned in for my Sports Writing course had solid reporting, but it lacked emotion.

This wasn't just another assignment. I built the course around a larger mission: reviving our dormant campus newspaper, *The Beacon*. In my six years teaching journalism at William Paterson, I never played a direct role in the paper, which prized its editorial independence. After the pandemic, though, *The Beacon* needed help. The paper had gone largely defunct, publishing only the occasional article, with no student editors or faculty adviser to recruit or guide new reporters.

The Sports Writing course became a platform to tie classwork to publication—tangible outcomes students could share with family, friends, and future employers. Never before had I taught a course that aligned so closely with both my passion as a fan and my research as a historian of sports media. If it worked, *The Beacon* would get a second life. If it didn't, our journalism students would lose one of the surest ways to secure the clips they needed to land internships and jobs.

I encouraged Matt to press the bowler about his childhood, reminding him that compelling journalism often demands respectful persistence.

My point resurfaced a few days later. Connie Chung, the longtime network anchor, was holding a book signing near campus, and I arranged a private meet-and-greet with my students afterward. Matt now had the chance to bring his questions about sensitive interview topics to a journalism legend.

In 1991, Chung conducted one of the most significant athlete interviews of all time: the first conversation with basketball superstar Magic Johnson after he announced his retirement from the NBA due to an HIV diagnosis. Chung was heralded for breaking news with empathy.

Standing beside his classmates in a strip-mall Barnes & Noble, Matt asked how Chung prepared for the interview. She told him it wasn't hard to come up with questions: How did Johnson get HIV? Was it from a man or a woman? Did his wife know?

"These questions are obvious," she told Matt, "because you just think about it, and what would any person want to know? You're the communicator who is asking for the information that you know your listener or viewer or reader will want answered."

Chung's message resonated with Matt. A reporter's primary obligation is to the public, and sometimes that involves asking provocative questions with care. As the evening wound down, Matt beamed while posing for photographs with Chung. He became one of the most consistent contributors to *The Beacon*. Now he's training to be its next editor in chief. That was exactly the kind of spark I hoped my course would ignite in students.

Clips are critical to the success of aspiring sports journalists. News outlets routinely ask applicants to submit examples of published work, and students without them risk losing out on career-altering opportunities (NBCU Academy, 2023). For many young reporters, landing a byline is so validating and motivating that it sparks deeper involvement in campus media (Renshaw, 2021). By simulating the pace and structure of a professional newsroom, campus newspapers help students develop the skills to report on deadline and adapt to fast-changing developments (Perry, 2023). Equally valuable, campus newsrooms serve as networking pipelines, connecting students with alumni who once reported for the same outlet and who now help successive generations secure internships and jobs (The Daily Tar Heel Alumni Association, n.d.; The Michigan Daily Alumni, n.d.).

The Beacon served this purpose for decades, evolving alongside its institution's changing identity and student population. Launched in 1936 as *The Paterson State Beacon*, the newspaper chronicled the transformation from a normal school to a teacher's college in 1937, a state college in 1971, and finally a university in 1997 (William Paterson University, n.d.-c). Over the decades, *The Beacon* published letters from students serving on the front lines in World War II, covered campus protests against U.S. involvement in Vietnam, and examined the wage gap between male and female faculty

Figure 10.1 Matt Goldman with former CBS News anchor Connie Chung at her book signing. Photograph by Nicholas Hirshon.

(Goldstein, 1972; Ross, 2006). A daring investigation in 1975 revealed that the university's president had allowed two thousand more students to enroll than permitted by the Department of Higher Education, ultimately leading to his resignation (Ross, 2006). *Beacon* alumni went on to prominent media careers, including a stock market reporter for CNN and the editor in chief of *Family Circle* (Stoll, 2011; Zecca, 2002). But in 2000, *The Beacon* came under fire for publishing an advertisement from a Holocaust denial group, followed by a parody issue laced with racial and religious stereotypes (Ross, 2006). The controversy prompted two journalism professors to launch a rival campus newspaper, and by the time I joined the faculty in 2016, *The Beacon* had been marginalized. Students were more drawn to the glitz of the radio and television stations. A decline in university enrollment meant fewer potential contributors. *The Beacon* lost its office in the student center, and the paper went defunct in 2022.

These setbacks reflected broader institutional challenges that reshaped who participated in campus media. The U.S. Department of Education designated William Paterson a Hispanic-Serving Institution (HSI) in 2014 (William Paterson University, n.d.-d). By 2025, the campus had become one of New Jersey's most diverse: 34.1% white, 30.3% Hispanic, 17.6% Black, 10.8% two or more races, and 6.9% Asian (William Paterson University, n.d.-a). Forty percent of our students are now the first in their families to attend college (William Paterson University, n.d.-c). For those balancing multiple jobs, unpaid reporting for a student newspaper may simply not be viable (Soria & Bultmann, 2014). Effective journalism can require late nights, emotional interviews, and deadline pressures, factors that can heighten stress and anxiety for students already juggling academic and financial burdens (Ogunrinde et al., 2025). In addition, campus newsrooms often skew upper middle class, making students from less affluent backgrounds feel out of place (Bettencourt, 2021).

I'm especially motivated to help my students overcome these barriers because campus media launched my own career. Clips from my college newspaper led to an internship at the *New York Daily News*, where I spent six years as a reporter before transitioning to teaching. I didn't want my students to lose that opportunity—especially at a time when their work could help fill the gap left by layoff-ravaged professional newsrooms across North Jersey.

As a first step to reviving *The Beacon*, I reached out in 2023 to the ReNews Project, a nonprofit organization that provides financial support and mentorship for student newspapers at HBCUs and HSIs. The group's executive director, Wesley Wright—a former reporter for the *Sun-Sentinel* and *Palm Beach Post*—stepped in as interim adviser. Gradually, a few stories began appearing on the website. However, Wright lived in Florida and could only advise students remotely. Much of campus life, including seven Division III teams and two club sports, remained uncovered.

This chapter serves as a guidebook for faculty at working-class universities to support campus media through coursework. It outlines practical steps to engage and empower students as journalists, reinforcing that their reporting matters on campus and beyond.

Reading the (Class)room

Teaching the Sports Writing course required assessing the students' backgrounds and interests. The class was small but diverse, with eight students spanning all stages of their college careers: two freshmen, one sophomore, four juniors, and one senior. Not all of them wanted to become sportswriters—four were journalism majors, while the others were studying sport management, sociology, and early childhood education. Two were student-athletes who would encounter the potentially awkward scenario of interviewing other student-athletes who were also their friends.

Meeting the needs and expectations of such a varied group called for creativity. Luckily, I had the freedom to adapt. Sports Writing was already in the course catalog, and the university-mandated outcomes were broad enough to support assignments for *The Beacon* without requiring new approvals or limiting instructional innovation. During the first class, I asked students to select William Paterson sports teams to cover for their beats. Each student would write three articles: a game story, a profile of a coach or player, and a feature. I then walked them through the process of composing an email to introduce themselves to the university's sports information director, or in the case of club sports, directly to the coach. Recognizing that some students would be more motivated to cover their favorite professional teams, I allowed them to write a column about a pro team of their choice, too.

Students quickly learned they needed to shift from fans to reporters, even though they naturally had a rooting interest in their own school. An early reading, Joe Gisondi's *Field Guide to Covering Sports*, emphasized the importance of neutrality and professionalism (Gisondi, 2017). I coached them to dress professionally—no William Paterson-branded clothing—and never cheer. I shared my own experience making that adjustment during my first college newspaper assignment. I had shown up to a swim meet wearing a hat with the university logo, and the sports editor told me to turn it around to avoid the appearance of bias. I wanted students to understand that many journalists before them, myself included, had gone through the same learning curve.

After laying the groundwork for campus reporting, I introduced students to *The Beacon*'s adviser. In addition to his time as a reporter, Wright had years of experience advising college reporters. The assistant director of student media at Florida Atlantic University in Boca Raton, Wright had also helped revive campus newspapers at Clark Atlanta University and Spelman College in Atlanta, Coppin State University in Baltimore, and Southern University in Baton Rouge, Louisiana. He had seen the challenges that students face in securing interviews and receiving pushback from sources, and he had grown familiar with the unique struggles at William Paterson.

Wright emphasized several lessons for new reporters. First, he encouraged students to regularly read journalism to grasp the mechanics of reporting and storytelling. He also addressed the common reluctance among students to pursue critical stories, explaining that covering a struggling team or athlete doesn't equate to negativity. "What I would caution you is, don't think of a story as negative," Wright told them. "Think of it as, 'OK, this happened. I have to report it.'" Finally, Wright underscored the importance of persistence and confidence in reporting, telling the class not to fear potential backlash from administrators. He reminded students that university employees are paid by taxpayer dollars and have a responsibility to answer questions. He assured them they certainly shouldn't be shy about approaching student-athletes, either. "It's not like it's the pope or Oprah or something," Wright said, drawing laughs. "They're regular people like you are. They're in class like you. They go to the dining hall like you do. Don't ever be afraid to say, 'Hey, I need help with this story. Are you open for an interview?'"

The students put Wright's advice into practice right away. I told the sports information director that my Sports Writing course would support *The Beacon*. He visited our class two days after Wright, advising students to provide advance notice when requesting interviews and outlining expectations for working with coaches and athletes.

Most students had never been exposed to the demands of a robust, probing student newspaper. The prospect had the potential to overwhelm them. But Wright had left them with encouraging advice: "Don't think there's any story that you can't do."

We marched on, with their first stories due in three weeks.

Inspiring Through Inclusion

The next several weeks of the course focused on inclusive storytelling. I told students that although William Paterson lacked the glamour of Division I athletics, our Division III teams likely had rich human-interest storylines that could be even more compelling, given the economic adversity many student-athletes face. I highlighted college journalism about underrepresented populations that might resonate at our majority-minority institution. Students read two powerful stories: one from the University of Miami about a star baseball player with autism (Schmelzinger, 2023), and another from Stanford University about the recruiting process for a baseball prodigy from Japan (Jing, 2024). These pieces underscored that sports writing goes beyond reporting box scores.

The next round of guest speakers also highlighted inclusive themes. A freelancer for the Golf Channel discussed his interview with Michelle Wie West, who spoke about her desire to grow women's golf (Schreiber, 2023). The host of a journalism podcast recounted meeting a Muslim college student who covered a Trump rally wearing her burqa and hijab: "She said, 'Yeah, I was nervous. Yeah, people pointed at me. Yeah, people took my picture. But I had made a decision that this is what I really wanted to do with my life, and I was not going to let something like that stop me.'" The point was clear: If that reporter could overcome that level of intimidation, my students could handle interviewing athletes and coaches on their own campus.

Student work started flowing in. The initial writing was rough, and some sourcing was thin, but the potential was unmistakable. One student profiled a DIII running back who took the unusual step of participating in intramurals during his recovery from injury (Nevels, 2024). Another wrote about an athlete who launched a podcast exploring the intersection of sports and Christian faith (Gonzalez, 2024). A third detailed the daily routine of the Zamboni driver at the arena where the university's hockey team plays (Horn, 2024).

With *The Beacon* lacking an active staff, I guided students through revisions and published the stories myself. They submitted their work through Blackboard, and I provided feedback based on reporting depth, writing clarity, and strength of sourcing. To mirror the copy flow of a professional newsroom, I gave them a final opportunity to revise before publication. I then shared the links with an advisory board of journalists I'd recruited and encouraged them to email the student authors with supportive feedback.

The students expressed surprise and excitement to receive validation from working journalists, and that propelled them through another wave of submissions tackling more critical topics. One student landed an interview with the football coach after a brutal 1–9 season (Sherwood, 2024). Another examined the bowling team's struggles under a new head coach, including candid quotes from athletes criticizing their leader for not being affirmative enough (Goldman, 2024). *The Beacon* was not publishing puff pieces; it was providing honest reporting.

My class earned a special treat at the end of the semester. I invited the communications manager from the NHL's New Jersey Devils to speak, and he arranged for my students to watch a game from the press box. Separately, I texted a friend who is a sportswriter and asked him to talk to the group about his job throughout the evening. After watching the Devils snap the Los Angeles Kings' six-game winning streak with a 3–1 victory, the class joined the media for the coach's post-game press conference. This experience fostered a renewed appreciation for sports journalism.

Conclusion

Linking coursework to publication in the Sports Writing course brought clear pedagogical benefits. Unlike assignments read only by a professor, these stories reached a broad audience—sources, classmates, faculty, and journalists on *The Beacon* advisory board—who offered constructive feedback and affirming praise. Knowing they were accountable to more than just me, students approached their reporting with greater purpose. Reporting a story couldn't be crammed into an all-nighter when students had to accommodate sources' schedules. They also needed to respond promptly to my edits, or risk having their byline appear on a version of the story they hadn't approved.

Still, the path to publication had obstacles. Students entered the course with wide-ranging skills and ambitions—some pursuing careers in sports media, others enrolling out of curiosity with no plans to become journalists. That made it harder to scaffold instruction in a way that addressed the full range of students' experiences and goals. I also had to balance the expectation of publication-ready articles with the reality that many working-class students—juggling part-time jobs that essentially amounted to full-time work—couldn't devote much time to reporting and writing. Without an active staff, I took on nearly all the responsibilities typically handled by student editors, from proofreading to publishing to promoting stories on

Instagram. I managed for a semester, but sustaining that pace alongside a 5–5 teaching load wouldn't be feasible.

Fortunately, I didn't have to maintain that intensity for long. The steady flow of new stories on *The Beacon* website inspired students to step up and take ownership. By spring 2025, *The Beacon* had assembled its first full editorial board in years. The newly energized team launched *The Beacon's* first-ever Spanish-language section and revitalized its Instagram with fresh reels. As the new staff got its bearings, I fed stories to *The Beacon* through a second course that I had pitched to the dean of the Honors College. I also advised two internal internships to guide the editor in chief and the news editor. Students began tackling tougher campus issues, including criticism of university fundraising practices and the decision to proceed with Black History Month events despite pressure from the Trump administration to scale back DEI initiatives. *The Beacon* leadership team remains shaky, with some contributors graduating and others hesitant to take on a full editor's workload. But for the first time in years, students are recruiting each other organically, without a professor driving the process.

Word of *The Beacon's* revival spread beyond campus. In the last week of the course, we welcomed a final guest speaker: John Byrne, a 1974 William Paterson graduate who served as editor in chief of *The Beacon* before rising to the same role at Fast Company and BusinessWeek.com. He told the students behind *The Beacon's* rebirth that his time at the paper changed his life. "*The Beacon* brought me out of my shell," he said. "It gave me a taste of what it would be like to manage people. But more importantly, it gave me a real taste for the impact that journalism can have."

Professors at working-class universities are uniquely positioned to spark the kind of transformation Byrne described. By creating opportunities for students to publish meaningful work, we can empower them to envision themselves on NFL sidelines and in MLB clubhouses.

In my course evaluations, students said my critiques improved their skills and confidence. They also voiced a desire for more guided, in-class writing exercises, which I intend to include the next time I teach the course.

After investing so much time into reviving *The Beacon*, I have some advice for instructors hoping to integrate coursework with student media. Most importantly, manage expectations and guard against burnout. Start with a single course, identify high-effort students to serve as editors and recruit others, and work closely with the editors to gradually shift editorial responsibilities back to them.

The Beacon is back on track—and students like Matt Goldman are poised to carry that momentum forward.

References

Bettencourt, G. M. (2021). "I belong because it wasn't made for me:" Understanding working-class students' sense of belonging on campus. *The Journal of Higher Education*, *92*(5), 760–783. https://doi.org/10.1080/00221546.2021.1872288

The Daily Tar Heel Alumni Association. (n.d.). *The Daily Tar Heel Alumni Association* [Facebook group]. Facebook. https://www.facebook.com/groups/29377572989/

Gisondi, J. (2017). From sports fan to sports reporter. In *Field guide to covering sports* (2nd ed., pp. 1–14). CQ Press.

Goldman, M. (2024, November 29). Bowling team, led by first new coach in 25 years, confronts losing, anonymity. The Beacon. https://wpubeacon.com/12712/sports/bowling-team-led-by-first-new-coach-in-25-years-confronts-losing-anonymity/

Goldstein, L. (1972, April 25). Rally clarifies Viet evils. *State Beacon*. https://repository.wpunj.edu/bitstream/20.500.12164/759/1/Beacon_1972-04-25.pdf

Gonzalez, J. (2024, November 27). Intramural athlete shares faith on Christian podcast. *The Beacon*. https://wpubeacon.com/12676/showcase/intramural-athlete-shares-faith-on-christian-podcast/

Horn, C. (2024, November 29). Ice Vault mainstay is more than just a Zamboni driver. *The Beacon*. https://wpubeacon.com/12694/uncategorized/ice-vault-mainstay-is-more-than-just-a-zamboni-driver/

Jing, K. (2024, August 17). How a Zoom call landed Stanford's next baseball phenom. *The Stanford Daily*. https://stanforddaily.com/2024/08/17/baseball-phenom-rintaro-sasaki/

The Michigan Daily Alumni. (n.d.). *The Michigan Daily Alumni* [Facebook group]. Facebook. https://www.facebook.com/groups/257657254267353/

NBCU Academy. (2023, May 17). Choose your best clips to get that news job. https://nbcuacademy.com/journalism-portfolio-articles/

Nevels, J. (2024, October 25). Intramural football part of return process for William Paterson running back. *The Beacon*. https://wpubeacon.com/12560/showcase/intramural-football-part-of-return-process-for-william-paterson-running-back/

Ogunrinde, J. O., Dang, P., Martins, L., Niazi-Galindo, N., Adepoju, O., & Mitchell, L. Y. (2025). Exploring the relationship between social demographic factors and anxiety in college students. *Journal of Affective Disorders Reports, 20*. https://doi.org/10.1016/j.jadr.2025.100896

Perry, A. (2023, December 1). How student and professional journalists are rewriting the industry pipeline. *The Objective*. https://objectivejournalism.org/2023/12/how-student-and-professional-journalists-are-rewriting-the-industry-pipeline/

Renshaw, M. (2021, February 17). Why it's worth catching the student news bug. *The Byline Club*. https://thebylineclub.wordpress.com/2021/02/17/why-its-worth-catching-the-student-news-bug/

Ross, T. E. (2006). *The Beacon*: Shining a light on the campus for nearly seventy years. *WP, 7*(1). https://www.wpunj.edu/news/assets/WP13.pdf

Schmelzinger, J. (2023, April 11). Ryland Zaborowski doesn't let autism stop him from crushing baseballs. *The Miami Student*. https://www.miamistudent.net/article/2023/04/ryland-zaborowski-doesnt-let-autism-stop-him-from-crushing-baseballs

Schreiber, M. (2023, May 6). Michelle Wie West: 'Would love for' women's game to keep growing without LIV Golf. *NBC Sports*. https://www.nbcsports.com/golf/news/michelle-wie-west-would-love-lpga-keep-growing-without-liv-golf

Sherwood, T. (2024, December 14). After 1–9 season, WP football team still sees hope. The Beacon. https://wpubeacon.com/12857/showcase/after-1-9-season-wp-football-team-still-sees-hope/

Soria, K. M., & Bultmann, M. (2014). Supporting working-class students in higher education. *NACADA Journal, 34*(2), 51–62. https://doi.org/10.12930/NACADA-13-017

Stoll, B. E. (2011). Susan Ungaro '75: Championing American cuisine. *WP, 12*(2). https://www.wpunj.edu/news/wpmagazine/pdfs/wpmag_fall11_onlinesmall.pdf

William Paterson University. (n.d.-a). *Current overall enrollment* [Data set]. https://app.powerbi.com/groups/me/apps/ff2c2453-4401-4422-b5dc-e4036ff69d82/reports/cf11e9b9-dae9-4a07-9e47-7a7c4a0eb5e9/ReportSection9619a149ba04100c5c5d?experience=power-bi

William Paterson University. (n.d.-b). *History of William Paterson University.* https://www.wpunj.edu/about-us/history/

William Paterson University. (n.d.-c). *University facts.* https://www.wpunj.edu/about-us/university-facts.html

William Paterson University. (n.d.-d). William Paterson University: A Hispanic-Serving Institution. https://www.wpunj.edu/about-us/hsi.html

Zecca, P. (2002). Susan Lisovicz: Reporting news is her business. *WP, 5*(1). https://www.wpunj.edu/news/assets/wp9.pdf

11 Partnering with Local and National News Organizations

Steve Fox,
University of Massachusetts at Amherst

If you're teaching sports journalism, you naturally will want to get students' work published. There are several ways to do that, and this chapter explores how to go about setting up partnerships between your sports journalism class and professional news organizations.

I founded the Sports Journalism Concentration at the University of Massachusetts about 10 years ago and I've taught a sports writing course for as long as I've been teaching at UMass. I started partnering up with news organizations quickly, and for the most part the arrangements have worked out well. In my news classes, students have had their work published in *The Boston Globe*, The Huffington Post and elsewhere while students in my sports classes have had their work published with ESPN.com, MassLive and *The Daily Hampshire Gazette*.

The First Steps

So, how to start? The keys are really finding the right partner and having the will as an instructor to make it work. When I first moved to Western Massachusetts, I made it a priority to get to know reporters and editors in the area. Over a few years I slowly developed relationships and got to a point where I felt I could work with an editor and an organization.

When developing an idea for a partnership, there are two critical first steps.

Step 1: Have story idea(s). Ideally you want students doing a combination of beat game coverage and feature stories and profiles. Even if students are working on feature stories, you want them attending practices and covering games.

Managing game stories and feature writing in one semester can seem daunting. Organization is key. In my class, the first class each week begins with a "News Meeting" where students divide up assignments for the week. In a class of 18, I usually have teams of three students covering different beats (usually high school football or other sports.) Over the course of the semester students are required to produce four or five game stories suitable for publishing, as well as a semester-long feature project and a couple of profiles.

A few years ago, students in my class spent the semester focused on producing profiles of women sports leaders to celebrate the anniversary of Title IX. The semester ended with all the stories published, but the success had a lot to do with the editor suggesting the story idea and working with students on the project over the course of the semester.

Over the years I've gone back and forth on whether to allow students to come up with story ideas. But I've found that going into the first week of class with a set project idea developed in conjunction with editors helps give the project an early kick start. A strong partner is key, which brings me to the second step.

Step 2: Find an editor. I've been lucky for the most part in that the editors I've worked with have been trustworthy and more than willing to spend time with students on reporting and writing issues that arise over the course of the semester projects. Developing trust is key in making the relationship work. Most working journalists want to work with students in developing stories that can be published. Often I will meet with the editors I'm working with over the course of the summer (for a Fall class) to talk over story ideas. Overworked editors often have a To-Do list of stories they want to get to but can't, and my class has been able to help on that front.

Trust, as we all know, is the backbone of our business. Players and coaches will not waste their time talking with student journalists unless there is trust. That trust also needs to be there with your newsroom partner.

As the instructor, you are the first line of defense when it comes to editing and fact checking. If students are writing game stories on deadline, instructors must rely on the expertise of their professional partners to make sure the story is suitable for publishing. I will back-read after stories are published and talk with students about any issues.

I take a more active editing role when it comes to the longer form profiles or feature stories. Those stories usually go through two-three drafts with me (and are graded) before being submitted to the editor for publication, where another level of editing will take place.

You also want to make sure that your partner doesn't "poach" stories produced by students. In most cases professionals will give credit via a "correspondent" or "contributor" byline, rewarding students for their hard work with a professional "clip" for their portfolio. I had a situation where a student in a news writing class had a scoop we shared with our professional partner. Without attribution to the student's work, the news organization took information for its own (lesser) version of the story. I ended the partnership immediately.

But I've also had very positive relationships. Jena Janovy, an ESPN.com editor and adjunct instructor in my department, took an interest in one student's story a few years ago and worked on fine-tuning it over a few months before it was published by ESPN.

Journalism departments and news organizations benefit tremendously from such partnerships. Students work directly with professional journalists and get their work published. News organizations get coverage and stories they might not necessarily be able to do without the assistance of students. Some view such partnerships as free labor, which is true, but you can only teach so much about sports journalism in the classroom. Students must get into the field (pun intended) to get a sense of what it's like to deal with players and coaches swimming through a sea of emotions in postgame interviews.

What students learn quickly is that covering sports involves a huge time commitment. I warn students repeatedly during the first week about the outside-of-class time requirement. Students committed to learning by doing find out about reality quickly. There is prep time: researching upcoming opponents and attending practices of the team you're covering. There is gathering material for previews as well as follow-ups, features and profiles.

And then there is game day coverage, which can last all day, depending on the sport. That's eye-opening to many students, along with the realization that they are covering games on nights and weekends—when all their friends are out partying.

Other Takeaways

Here are a few other key takeaways I've learned about classroom partnerships with news organizations.

Instructor Workload

Sure, the class is a lot of work for students but there's no way around it: Your teaching workload grows when you take on a partnership. In many ways the classroom dynamic evolves from instructor-student roles to the more familiar editor-reporter relationship we see inside newsrooms.

That evolution naturally means a much larger time commitment on your part. You're working with students outside of class as well as in-class and they are (hopefully) reaching out to you with questions. The biggest stressor for educators is making sure that what they publish is accurate—worries that can lead to more than a few sleepless nights.

The workflow for students can be a bigger challenge. In my class of 16 to 18 students, I will usually have a handful who are doing internships and/or student media while also taking a full class load. A partnership class like this definitely tests students' time management skills. As a friend of mine reminded me, the class workload gives students an idea of the commitment involved in a career as a sports journalist.

Deadlines

Perhaps the biggest lesson with these partnerships is training students to write effectively on deadline. When covering some games, students sometimes have only an hour to conduct postgame interviews, write and file their stories. No classroom deadline can match that of an adrenaline-filled Friday night high school football game and writing against a deadline.

Having said that, I'm a bit more flexible with their larger project work. I want them producing their best journalism, so I try to give students the time needed to do that before submitting for publication.

Communication

I've used many different tools over the years—ranging from Facebook groups to Slack—to stay in touch with students and partner editors. And while I hesitate to give my phone number to students, this class is the one exception, and students will text me when issues arise.

In one instance, a team of students were covering a high school basketball game when a fire broke out in another part of the school, forcing the gym to be evacuated. One student texted me and asked if they should do a story on the fire. My response was "of course," and they ended up with a front-page story on the fire the next day along with the game story.

The other part of the communication puzzle is staying in touch with the respective editors you work with. I've been lucky to work with sports editors who really care about working with and teaching students. They viewed their work with students as a way to give back, and they certainly do that and more.

Case Studies

Over the years I've connected with sports journalism educators who also find ways to get their students to work with professional journalists. Those of us who teach in this space are a pretty tight-knit group, and I always find time for those teaching sports at various academic conferences. I've chosen a few programs and their respective instructors as case studies.

The University of Georgia

I get exhausted after listening to Mark E. Johnson and Vicki Michaelis talk about their sports partnerships with their students. (Full disclosure: I've known Johnson for more than 10 years and pick his brain often for ideas.)

Michaelis is the director of University of Georgia's John Huland Carmical Sports Media Institute at UGA, while Johnson directs the photojournalism program at UGA. Both have extensive backgrounds as professional journalists, with Michaelis spending more than a dozen years at *USA Today* covering the Olympics and other sports while Johnson's resume includes stints with the Associated Press.

For years they, along with professors and students at Penn State University, have provided coverage for the Associated Press at major sporting events. Most recently Johnson and colleague Welch Suggs accompanied nine students to Paris to provide coverage at the 2024 Paralympics, and in 2023 another 17 attended the Women's World Cup in Australia. Planning for these trips usually begins at least a year beforehand, with prospective students going through an exhaustive tryout process about nine months before the events. The collaborations aren't formal classes, but many students use the experience as part of their program capstone.

AP editors have consistently been impressed with the work produced by UGA students, and Michaelis also stressed the importance of developing strong relationships with their AP partners.

"You have to know and trust the editors and they have to know and trust you," said Michaelis in an interview.

Managing expectations with editors as well as students is also a key component when setting up these projects. Johnson said that students need to understand that they are attending these events to work, not play, and that understanding how to manage life on the road is a key component during the selection process. Jet lag, sleep, diet, and exercise are the parts of life that can become a challenge for sports journalists on the road. Students quickly learn the importance of time management.

The expectations game is also something to take into account when dealing with professional partners.

"You need editors who understand that the students aren't going to be able to drop in as stringers and deliver just exactly what they need," said Michaelis. "So you need to have these open communications with the editors about what your students can bring."

Editors also learn pretty quickly the level of work that students can produce, which "quickly changes their perspective," says Johnson. Students provide a different approach to coverage, Johnson added, which is deeply appreciated by AP editors.

Being in the field at such major events can be intimidating for even the most confident student photojournalist. And getting questions answered at postgame scrums/press conferences can be a huge challenge for student writers. But Johnson found that many professional journalists will reach out and give a helping hand to students.

Essentially, Johnson and Michaelis are seeking to give students the experience of covering a major sports event without the hectic scrums we're all familiar with. By choosing the Paralympic Games over the Olympics and the group-play matches over elimination matches at the Women's World Cup, students are able to avoid being overrun by professional journalists.

"Our approach is to go where the crowds aren't," said Michaelis. "This means the photojournalists don't have to battle for photo positions. It means the writers have a better shot at accessing sources in the mixed zone and open locker rooms and at getting their questions answered in press conferences. The learning experience in these environments is much better than at events where our students get crowded out, relegated to cherry-picking quotes."

The University of Georgia is fortunate to have two dedicated and inspiring professors running this program, but the students are also fortunate to have the bulk of the costs for such collaborations taken care of. Currently, students chosen to take part in these trips only pay for airfare and some meals when they're on the ground. Michaelis explained that she and Johnson maintain an ethos where they do not undertake these projects unless they've received funding to cover most of the costs, which usually comes from several sources.

"We tell the students not to let costs stop them from trying out for this," said Johnson.

What's interesting about professional-classroom collaborations is that students not only learn how to operate under deadline conditions but there are some who realize that the lifestyle is not for them. After the Australia trip, Johnson was told by two student journalists that they did not see journalism in their future.

"That's still a good learning outcome, better to learn that at 21," said Johnson.

When teaching on-the-ground in Athens, Michaelis manages the stresses of student sports journalists, letting students know that sources not returning phone calls or rainouts messing with personal schedules is all part of the job. She says that international trips just add another layer to that.

"I'm trying to put you in a situation that is as real as it can be so you can see whether this is something you want to pursue," said Michaelis. "I'm not here to hold your hand but to put you out there and see if you like it."

The Ohio State University

At both the college and professional levels, sports writers seek access to players and coaches. To do that, sports writers must work through, with and around sports information directors and media relations professionals. As with all professional relationships, getting cooperation from public relations professionals means earning their trust—which takes time and finesse.

It can be tough to teach and especially difficult for students to learn how to develop that trust with PR professionals in one semester. When Nicole Kraft started teaching sports journalism at The Ohio State University, first on her to-do list was meeting with the athletic director and the university's Sports Information Directors (SIDs) with the hopes of smoothing out access issues for student journalists.

Now, while some may think getting cooperation from officials at a renowned athletics program like that one at Ohio State might be difficult, Kraft's message was a simple one: "You do athletics at the highest level. I want to make reporters who work at the highest level. Let's put on a show together."

Kraft is aware of athletic directors who have an inflated sense of their position and need to control press accessibility—even at small or mid-size programs. The athletic directors and SIDs she works with understand that teaching is part of their mission as well, even at THE Ohio State University.

"We did win the national championship this year [the 2024 football season], and our doors could not be more open," said Kraft.

Kraft's background as a sports journalist helped her sell the idea to the OSU athletic director but she also presented her syllabus and class goals. And, perhaps most importantly, Kraft said she would be with her students "every step of the way." Kraft's teaching style is hands-on, and she attends games, practices and media availability with students—a task she considers critical in teaching students how to behave in an environment where almost everyone is cheering.

"They learn quickly what is professional behavior," said Kraft, who has taken up to 21 students to cover a football game. "Inevitably there is one (student) who claps in the press box, and everyone looks at them and it never happens again."

She also enlists their help, as well as that of college athletes to run mock press conferences where athletes and university officials give feedback on student questions and performance. This intriguing element to Kraft's classes allows students to learn and make mistakes while practicing with public relations officials, preparing them for when they are in a live press conference.

Kraft also created a media relations course, which in turn helps out those in the athletic department. She also works to place students in internships with professional teams in Columbus. While her background is in covering professional sports, Kraft has learned the parameters of college sports—parameters which continue to shift, thanks to NIL.

"Most of our coaches are committed to teaching people," she said.

As for the time commitment, Kraft admits there is a heavy workload, but, as she says, "I would be going to sports anyways."

Springfield College

Springfield College is about 20 minutes down Interstate 91 from UMass Amherst, where Marty Dobrow has been teaching sports journalism for more than 20 years. Dobrow's main connection with newsrooms and their sports desks is through internships with local news organizations, public access television as well as The Boston Globe and ESPN. There is an internship requirement in the department and students there regularly do multiple internships.

Dobrow is the internship coordinator and supervises the internships via a class every semester. He relies heavily on the site supervisors and stays in touch with them to check on students' progress.

That type of regular check-in also requires strong relationships with editors, and Dobrow contributes a significant amount of time tracking the progress of his students.

"We have developed some pretty good partnerships, pretty reliable ones," including both print and online publications, Dobrow said. "The quality of those experiences hinges significantly on what type of supervision students are getting on site. We're a small operation so I'm not going to be able to go out and visit students on site."

The internship experience is often what students make of it. As with any newsroom, raising your hand and offering to cover games instead of just working the phones is the type of behavior we all try to instill in our students. About 12 students take the internship class each semester, and Dobrow has students journal their experiences as another way of tracking how they're faring.

"It's not just a 'write-anything' journal," said Dobrow. "I do think a lot of learning can come through reflection."

A good number of his students end up either getting hired where they intern or otherwise engage. The one consistent finding with professional partnerships is that programs whose students interact with professionals in internships almost always have a positive outcome.

Dobrow and others say the biggest factor is how much effort the students put into the internship experience. The one concern many departments face is whether to advocate for unpaid internships. Many sports internships are unpaid, but the question of free labor has to be balanced with the experience gained.

These examples are just a handful of many efforts happening at journalism programs around the country. And as newsrooms continue to downsize, I imagine these opportunities will grow. It may sound a bit odd, but one major benefit to having young aspiring sports writers covering high schools and colleges is their youth. They bring excitement but they can also relate to young players. As student-athletes continue to control their Name, Image and Likeness, young sports writers can and should be able to relate to their stories—and then tell them.

As sports journalism instructors, our role really is more of an editor and using the skills we have honed to help students get published is a major benefit to our students. My advice? Start small and grow over time. Understand and embrace the workload. And revise and update as you move forward. As with sports journalism, teaching in this format is never boring and is ever changing.

Part IV
Teaching Ideas Bigger Than the Game

12 Teaching Courageous Sports Conversations as They Intersect with Race, Gender, and Class

Claire Smith and Karen M. Turner, Temple University

Engaging in courageous, knowledgeable conversations when sports media intersect with sensitive topics like race, gender, class, religion, and other critical issues is a key component of the Klein College of Media and Communication's sports curriculum at Temple University. The teaching of thoughtful, respectful exploration of these interconnected subjects in a safe classroom space is why *The Influence of Sports Media on Modern Society* was designed as a mandatory course for the Klein Certificate in Sports Media, launched in 2021.

The course was originally conceived and taught by Professor Karen M. Turner in Spring 2021, when most offerings were held online because of COVID-19. Despite the challenges of virtual instruction, student feedback from that first cohort helped Turner enhance and refine the course for its in-person debut in Fall 2021.

Spring 2022, Turner teamed up with Claire Smith to co-teach the course. This arrangement paired Turner's decades of teaching experience with Smith's celebrated background as a pioneering Major League Baseball writer and columnist.

The Influence of Sports Media on Modern Society being taught by two trailblazing Black women added significance to the students' experience— infusing the course with powerful meaning through both representation and connection. Their presence enriched not only the course content but also the context in which it was delivered, allowing students to engage more authentically. Centered around sport—a universal activity that bridges diverse communities—the course uses current events as a dynamic entry point for open, honest, and often challenging conversations about the intersection of race, gender, class, identity, and society.

Turner, a seasoned professional in both media and academia, has been instrumental in shaping this course and in fostering a culture of inclusion at Temple University's Klein College of Media and Communication. As a member of Dartmouth College's first class of women to matriculate as freshmen, she has long navigated the intersections of race and gender in her own educational journey, professional media experience and academic career, bringing invaluable perspective to the classroom.

Smith, enjoying her first go-round in education, spent over 45 years breaking barriers in sports media, with the bulk of her experience compiled while covering baseball for *The New York Times, The Philadelphia Inquirer* and ESPN, among other outlets. Along the way, the inaugural member of The Black Sportswriters' Hall of Fame won the Associated Press Sports Editors' Red Smith Award and the Baseball Writers' Association of America's Career Excellence Award. As you will see in some of the case studies that will follow, her interest in the way baseball intersects with society followed her to Temple. The sport of Jackie Robinson and the many athlete activists that followed Robinson offers focal points offered by guest lecturers. Whether Turner's and Smith's impressive lineup of guests visit the classroom or Temple's Claire Smith Center for Sports Media, the professors use these opportunities to prompt students to engage in dialog about the intersection of sports and society.

Notable guests, who joined virtually or in-person to share their insights and experiences have included, ESPN's Howard Bryant and Kevin Negandhi, Yankees broadcaster Suzyn Waldman, renowned sportscaster Bob Costas, Temple University women's basketball head coach Diane Richardson, and MLB Players Association Executive Director Tony Clark.

Within years of establishing *The Influence of Sports Media on Modern Society,* Turner has watched as the course took on added significance by 2025. Not only is it a requirement for Klein College of Media and Communication students seeking a Sport Media Certificate, but it will also be required for the college's Sports Media major, launching in July 2025.

As envisioned by the now-emerita Turner, exploring issues beyond the game is a core aspect of the course, regardless of students' majors. Whether they're pursuing careers in print or digital sports reporting, or content creation roles for athletes, teams, or leagues, students in *The Influence of*

Sports Media on Modern Society are encouraged to recognize that many of the most significant challenges they will face won't revolve around the X's and O's of any one game, season, or sport.

Beginning on the first day of class, students are instructed to identify current sports events pertaining to a range of societal issues such as the pandemic, race, gender, social class, sexual identity, religion and politics. Students were informed that this would be the format for the start of each class. This approach heightened their awareness of how sports intersect with these societal issues beyond the classroom. For example, students brought into the classroom, stories such as the New Jersey high school wrestler forced to cut his dreadlocks to compete, as well as the first openly transgender University of Pennsylvania swimmer, who won an NCAA Division I national championship.

During the first week, students are also asked to complete an introductory assignment with two main goals. First, it allows the professors to get to know the students by exploring their media consumption habits—what they read, watch, and listen to—as well as their career goals. Second, it provides insight into the students' initial perspectives on how societal issues intersect with sports, and how effectively they believe sports media address these intersections.

Throughout the semester, students discussed topics that left some feeling uncomfortable. Recognizing this, Smith and Turner emphasized the importance of modeling vulnerability and stepping beyond *their own* comfort zones. The students also understood that classroom discussions would be kept confidential.

Fully assuring that classroom discussions occur in a safe and respectful space remains tantamount. The emphasis to students that everything shared within the bounds of propriety stays within the classroom has taken on new weight in today's political climate. Educators cannot be oblivious to the shifting political currents. With increasing scrutiny over course content, including grant challenges, lawsuits, and the targeting of institutions and individual instructors, even seasoned teachers may begin to question their ability—or authority—to facilitate these crucial conversations on complex and sometimes volatile topics.

The Influence of Sports Media on Modern Society is now being taught at a time when the federal government has under scrutiny academic programs, course content, and the makeup of student bodies and staff. Officials in charge of grants, visas for foreign students and educators, are using their power like cudgels, insisting more and more that colleges and universities limit thought, issues, even words. If one does not know the consequences of saying "diversity," "equity" or "inclusion," for reasons of policy or debate, it is logical to think that such words—and the discussions that might accompany them—may be silenced.

Case Study 1: The Value of Group Projects when Building Collaboration

In Spring 2022, Smith and Turner introduced what is now a course staple: The Group Project. Students are guided through the process that will lead to a project worth, and worthy of, one-fifth of a student's grade.

The expectations for such projects are first shared during the reading of the syllabus in Week 1's two sessions. The directions, ideas and fundamentals of what is expected by the end of a 15-week semester is constantly underscored through the Canvas LMS "Assignments," "Announcements" and "Module" tabs in course-related on-line instructions, in-class consultations and in-person project proposal reviews.

Once groups are formed and topics are approved, dates are set for proposal presentations. These proposals are shared with the class and professors for feedback during scheduled sessions, which serve as dress rehearsals. The Q&A that follows—between students and professors—helps identify whether any adjustments to the topic or the group's approach to the subject matter are necessary. Approximately two months later, final presentations take place on Exam Day. Each group then has one additional day to submit a revised final version, incorporating feedback from both peers and professors.

The Group Project assignment measures how well student teams interpret given sports media/societal issues. They must craft timelines and adhere to deadlines both individually and within the group over the course of the second half of the 15-week semester.

Students are measured by how well they listen to, learn from, and work with each other. Each student is challenged to hone their reportorial, editorial, media and communication skills. They must help coordinate a class presentation that serves as their class final (worth one-fifth of the final course grade).

Why the Group Projects instead of written finals? Such assignments are always challenging to students, who must ascertain the strengths and, yes, weaknesses of each member, utilize the observations, then design the team and delivery methods accordingly.

To assist in navigating the process, Smith and Turner identified a "leader" in each group, who served as point person with the instructors.

During the creation of the projects, students were encouraged to focus on the process itself. Each group had access to its own discussion board, collaboration tools, and calendar. Regular meetings to discuss the topic were crucial. Each group was expected to establish and follow a clear approach to the subject, working inductively by first gathering articles and other materials related to the topic's questions. Additionally, students were asked to work deductively, starting with a specific focus and then collecting relevant resources for the project.

The inductive approach works best when the group is unsure about the focus or questions. However, choose the approach that best suits the group's needs. The timeline should include scheduled consultation dates with the professor. The professor will help the group recognize the value of stepping outside their comfort zones to gain new insights and will encourage discussions that might not happen if the group only follows safe paths toward the common goal.

By the end of the course, it is hoped that the students understand the true nature of this crowning finale. This Group Project exercise is designed to add invaluable insights for students seeking to one day work within media professions that require partnerships, collaborative skills and appreciate the value of shared goals and responsibilities. Also, as important, after working together, each student should have a greater appreciation for keeping an open mind, thinking outside safe zones and valuing diverse approaches and opinions.

Group Project: 75th Anniversary of Jackie Robinson Breaking into Major League Baseball

The overarching focus for each group in this 2022 class was the impact of sports and race on society. Each group researched one of the various angles of the moment a Black American was permitted to play Major League Baseball, thus smashing the game's half-century-old color barrier. Smith and

Turner developed relevant topics for the groups to explore Jackie Robinson's move to the Brooklyn Dodgers in 1947. The six topics were:

· Getting the call: Why Jackie Robinson? This group was asked to examine how socioeconomics, national and international geo-political winds, the post-war impact, education differences between American societies North, South and West of the Mason Dixon Line, helped drive decisions as to how we would integrate.

· Blacks in baseball: Is a group who looked at the roots found in the Civil War, the Negro Leagues' impact through the mid-20th Century, re-integration of the game, the Golden Age of African American baseball (Willie Mays, Hank Aaron, Frank Robinson, Billy Williams), and the erosion of the game's claim to being the national pastime of both Black and white America.

· Jackie Robinson and the City of Brotherly Love: Being in Philadelphia, it was important that the students explored the ugliness, and open racism that greeted Robinson in his first encounter with the Phillies.

· The Media in Black and White: Students in this group were asked to research how the sports media of the day covered Jackie Robinson, and the role played by historically Black publications.

· The Shattering of Other Glass Ceilings in Baseball: Students were tasked with focusing on gender equality in a game that has long been dominated by white men. They were to look from press boxes, to the appointment of the sport's first female general manager, to female pioneers, including women of color.

· Activism in Baseball: This group had an interesting assignment due to athlete activism today. When the public thinks about Jackie Robinson, it's usually about his baseball career. However, Smith and Turner thought to bring the Jackie Robinson story full circle, it was important for the group to research his activities once he put down his bat. He was an advocate for equal opportunities as managers, coaches, GM positions and other key spots in the baseball management hierarchy. Jackie's controversial siding with Curt Flood for the civil rights of workers in uniform illustrated the part his role played in what became pro sports' most powerful labor movement. And students were tasked to look at other methods of activism such as ownership. Before Jackie Robinson, there was Effa Manley, a Negro Leagues team owner and

Civil Rights advocate who is the only woman inducted into The Baseball Hall of Fame.

Another Group Example

In another example of the group process, in the following semester, Fall 2022, the Group Project focused on ideas taken from answers in the introductory assignment. The students were told that in the introductory assignment they were asked, "Is there a sport that you'd like to study in more depth to discover its impact on our society?" This group assignment is based on those responses.

We created five Sport Discussion Groups: College basketball (men's/women's), NBA, WNBA, baseball, and football.

Students were told: "Through this assignment you will look into the history of the sport, key movers and shakers (players, sports journalists, owners, others) and how the sport has influenced aspects of society, good and not so good. For example, the baseball group could look at the history and societal impact of the All-American Girls Professional Baseball League or women owners in the Negro Leagues."

Case Study 2: Documentaries as 21ˢᵗ Century Teaching Tools

With each click, each like, each smiling emoji, many members of the younger generations driving modern media usage cast their votes in favor on how they choose to consume news, sports, and entertainment. Tik-Tok, YouTube, and countless streaming platforms live where kids' do—in the world of the audio-visual. That educators would be wise to acknowledge the increasingly obvious: The written word may not be passe, but textbooks, newspapers and magazines have dwindled in influence in some classroom structures. Documentaries are nestling into those vacated spaces as viewing assignments becomes as integral to some curricula as reading assignments.

This has certainly become the case in *The Influence of Sports Media on Modern Society*. The course leans heavily into these changing seas, using documentaries to draw students into a subject's story in more three-dimensional ways. Motion pictures are not new, but the growth industry of sports docs is quite frankly enjoying a golden age, as streaming platforms provide compelling stories in their own interpretations of reality TV.

Every word said in ESPN's debut *Nine for IX* documentary *Venus Vs.* ... could have been printed in 60-point type. Instead, it was filmed, with its emotions and plot build-ups by director Ava DuVernay. The film features tennis icon Venus Williams and her groundbreaking fight for equal prize money for women at Wimbledon. Her story is told through archival footage, interviews, and personal reflections. The documentary focuses on how Williams used her international platform to advocate for change—including the writing of a powerful op-ed in *The Times* of London that criticized the tournament for its refusal to pay women equally. Her efforts ultimately helped lead to Wimbledon finally granting equal prize money. Wimbledon was the last of the four major Grand Slam tennis tournaments to offer pay parity to men and women. The 2013 documentary highlights many of the issues studied in this sports course, not just money, but race, equity, gender bias, class, and inclusion. This documentary also highlights the unique pressures faced by an accomplished Black woman challenging the status quo in a white, male-dominated sport.

The video was compelling, and its staying power was proven by how often students referred to it during the 15-week class. Many acknowledged never having heard of Venus, let alone her campaign that won its final victory at Wimbledon. By showing Venus raising the winner's trophy in 2007—the same Wimbledon tournament in which the British finally raised women's prize money to equal the men—was powerful and not lost on the class.

The lesson did not end with the closing credits. Students were asked to reflect on the lessons learned by submitting answers to prompts and questions posed on the Canvas Discussion Board by Smith and Turner. They included:

- Identify the social issues highlighted in the film.
- Identify any that were not explored but could be relevant to the story or not explored in-depth. How would you have brought one of these issues into the story?
- How would a childhood residence in Beverly Hills as opposed to Compton impact Venus on issues of equity?
- Did any male athletes show allyship? If so, how?
- Do you think Venus seemed more comfortable as an activist than Serena? Explain.

- What's the overall message of the documentary?
- Fill in the blank: If you were to finish the title of this story it would be *Venus vs…* what/who? And why?

The students shared their responses as part of an in-class exercise. In doing so, they saw that their answers revealed shared insights, an appreciation of history that no longer seemed ancient, and the fact that everything old is new, again. After all, what Venus fought for was playing out again, as salary discrepancies between the men and women in pro basketball and USA soccer showed how gender bias wasn't left behind in the 20th Century. And the students were reminded that such bias and inequity are not limited to sports.

Other issues, such as the "words hurt" aspect led to examination of how Venus and her sister, Serena, were stereotyped. The two Black girls from Compton, California, were shown being humiliated and held to different standards, reducing the teenaged Venus to tears at times.

Such insensitive treatment of two girls of yesteryear made today's students feel uncomfortable. Those reactions themselves spoke to how empathy can be one of the most important lessons of all after you literally hear and see a subject's pain on the screen.

Smith and Turner applied a similar approach when transitioning to the LGBTQ+ module, particularly when discussing the complex issue of transgender athletes. It was evident that some students were grappling with their perspectives. To facilitate a judgment-free discussion, Smith and Turner introduced the 2016 ESPN documentary, *Life as Matt*, to engage the class. When available, we also invited Matt and his mom to campus to participate in the discussion.

Case Study 3: Dealing with a Controversial or Contentious Issue—"Shut Up and Dribble"

Throughout the semester, Smith and Turner explored various ways to keep students engaged. One of the most popular activities was in the "activism in sports" module that challenged their creativity and pushed them outside their comfort zones. Students were asked to take a stance on an issue with which they might not agree, prompting them to critically examine their views.

In February 2018, Fox News host Laura Ingraham sparked controversy when she told NBA superstar LeBron James, along with other athletes, to "shut up and dribble" after they criticized then-President Donald Trump. James was known for his outspoken views on social and political issues. In this instance, he criticized Trump's rhetoric and policies. Ingraham responded, saying that athletes should stay in their own entertainment lane and not offer political advice. She famously stated she wasn't going to take political advice from "someone who gets paid $100 million a year to bounce a ball."

This incident was met with divided public opinions. Some agreed with Ingraham, arguing that athletes should not use their celebrity platforms to address political and social issues. Others, however, believed that athletes, like any other citizens, had the right to speak on matters of public concern. The controversy highlighted the intersection of race, politics, class, and sports.

Since the "shut up and dribble" controversy was familiar to most students, Smith and Turner developed an in-class exercise inspired by the law school Moot Court format. The students were randomly divided into three groups. One group was tasked with defending the "Shut up and Dribble" perspective, while another group took the position of "Take a Knee," arguing in favor of Colin Kaepernick's silent protest. The third group served as judges.

Each of the two participating groups was given flip chart paper and markers to develop their arguments within half the class time. Meanwhile, the judges' group met to assign a head judge who would lead the deliberation.

At the end of the allotted time, the groups came together to present their arguments and answer questions from the judges. The judges then deliberated. Upon reconvening the class, the winning group was announced, and the judges explained their decision.

In most semesters, the judges consistently chose the "Shut up and Dribble" group as the winner. They noted that this group seemed more passionate arguing that athletes should stay out of off-court/field controversies. Perhaps this is due to defending a stance they might not normally agree with in real life. These debates sparked discussions within the class about comfort zones and prompted students to reflect on their own unconscious biases.

An example of group positions:

Take a Knee: (pro athlete activism)

- Forces people to pay attention
- They're human, too
- Athletes have First Amendment rights and should use their platform

- Shut up and dribble: (con athlete activism)
- Abusing their own power
- Sports are made for entertainment
- Sports and politics don't mix
- Turns fans away.

During recent semesters, students were asked to delve into not just their own memories of the consequences of athletes taking either stance. They were given chapters to read in "It Was Always a Choice," in preparation for question & answer sessions with guest lecturer David Steele, the book's author. Assigned chapters included the history of athletes' activism during the nation's Jim Crow era in which "gentlemen's agreements" segregated not only sports, but the nation in every facet of life.

The students asked Steele questions about the known activists (Jackie Robinson, Muhammad Ali, Bill Russell, Venus Williams) and the famously apolitical star players (Michael Jordan, Charles Barkley). The students' questions predominantly came from an area of wanting to know more rather than having Steele confirm already formed opinions. That underscored the importance of exposing each generation to the lesser known aspects of history, as well as illustrating how sports, race and culture have always intertwined and impacted changes in an ever-evolving American society.

Conclusion

The course *The Influence of Sports Media on Modern Society* holds even greater significance today, as courageous discussions on race, gender, class, and other 'isms are increasingly being stifled. As societal priorities shift, so too does the course content—so no two semesters are the same. This evolving landscape keeps the course both timely and relevant.

Every semester, we explore core themes, including sports history, race and gender issues, media bias, mental health in athletics, activism, allyship, and LGBTQ+ representation. Depending on current events and student interest, we've also examined topics such as sports betting, Name-Image-Likeness (NIL) rights, globalization, and ageism in sport.

We have learned that facilitating courageous conversations requires us, as instructors, to step beyond our own comfort zones and model what we want from the students. Demonstrating authenticity, honesty, and vulnerability sets the tone for the kind of dialogue we hope to inspire in our students. Building a safe and trusting classroom environment takes time. We often reserve the most challenging and potentially sensitive topics until a strong sense of mutual respect and comfort has developed among the class. Sports, in particular, offers a unique platform where people from diverse backgrounds can unite. Therefore, it's essential for journalism students to be exposed to these critical issues.

13 Using Sports Media to Teach Social Theory

Michael Mirer,
University of Wisconsin-Milwaukee

I work in a professionally focused media program—not sports specific—where the emphasis is on helping students develop practical skills. In their major coursework, our students are usually learning how to write leads, press releases, and creative briefs. All of this is important. But media professions do not exist in isolation. Journalism and persuasive media fields speak to shared ideas and social norms. Learning how to write a lead without understanding how we make choices about what belongs in a lead and how those choices affect our readers leaves students half prepared. I know from our early semester conversations that many of my media students feel suspicious of or intimidated by theory. The power of teaching classes that look at the interfaces between sports, media, and society is that we help our students get their hands around these concepts and apply them in the media they are already consuming. The point of social theory is that it predicts how people and institutions work in real life. By placing media and social theory in a sports context, we can push our students not just to consume the ideas but to search for expressions of them (or their absence) in media content. My goal here is to take the habits they have developed in a professional-skills focused education and use them to make the abstractions of theory more concrete.

Sports, media, and society courses can take many forms. Some are large introductory lectures that serve as a front door for many of our programs. Others are parts of sports media major or program requirements. My course is a smaller seminar, one that fulfills the campus research writing requirement. Many of my students want to work in sports. Some are already interning at our city's local teams. It is a discussion-based course that has between 16–20 students depending on the semester and number of students who are on the cusp of graduation. For our students the seminar they take often requires a refresher in scholarly writing and research that they have fallen out of practice with. The main output is a research paper, which I also treat as a form of professional writing. There is no magic or mystery in media analysis. It is about developing a question and then going about answering it in a systematic way. That is what many of us do in research roles too. If they are practicing being a professional in their other classes, they can do the same with me. That said, most know they do not want to be academics.

Teaching the Need to Think Deeply About Sports

One consistent challenge is getting students to see the value in the work we are doing in this class. I start from the perspective that critique is about deep engagement, not necessarily about finding the fault in sports or sports media. Taking a more analytical approach to sports is a soft skill; it is the reconciling of complexity and thinking critically as they prepare for their roles. Part of professionalism is not just being able to do basic things, but also the ability to speak knowledgeably about your corner of the world. It is why most professional media programs require some attention to media ethics. As a former journalist and journalism instructor myself, I know the ways we teach students to report and to write are tied directly to a vision of the role of truth and ethical discourse in society. This is a necessity in sports media programs as well. What I want them to think about is what sports and sports media do in society. It is my job to introduce those ideas and it is their job to consider them. My students see the clear application of developing communication plans in their PR classes but often have a harder time grasping why social identity theory might matter to them. Yet we are awash in sports content, and we can find examples of team communication pitched to creation of a fandom as in-group or a reflection of civic cohesion.

The second challenge is related. A student who opts for a sports communication class—or, indeed, a sport media major—is not walking in with the mindset of a critical sociologist. I have heard many sports journalism professors lament that their students are more interested in the "sports" than the "journalism." Given that we understand how message framing affects people, we should not be surprised when our sports-interested students tell us they want to work in this area because it is a break from the real world.

They learn this from watching sports, the lofty ways athletes, broadcasters, and officials attempt to position sports as something that transcends the drudgery of politics and struggle. Most of us who teach and research sports media in higher education have grown out of the uncritical love for the spectacles many of our students are so eager to get close to. We have read media sociology and produced studies that show how sports, often through the choices made by media producers of many stripes, can be engines for the reproduction of inequalities, stereotypes, and other social ills. Our students have not. In speaking across that divide, we are introducing them to the ideas they need for careers in sports or sports-adjacent media, while also encouraging them to move toward disillusionment at their own pace. I have heard colleagues say that their students say that thinking critically has ruined sports for them. I suppose that can happen. But I also know that students resist that. And my own moral clarity is useless in a classroom if it stops the students from considering the ideas I believe they need to be successful and ethical as members of a professional community. My own approach has been to be open about my own sports fandom and enjoyment. I illustrate my own points with examples from my own life to express my own comfort with the contradictions. It helps, perhaps, that I do not believe sports have any intrinsic meaning. The projection of values into sports and of sporting values into other contexts are communicative efforts. And we can identify that in content and show students how to apply communication theory to how that context works.

Working from the Inside Out

As such, my approach to teaching sports and society is to work from the media industry outward. The earliest course materials focus on the construction and remaking of the media system and how that connects to broader societal shifts. The starting point for my sports, media, and society classes is to think through what comprises the sports media today. Pedagogically it is important for them to think about the collective noun "media" to understand the ways different outlets serve distinct audiences. Thinking about the ways professions fit into that system is usually a place they are eager to start. For systems, my primary tactic of this has been to project Lawrence Wenner's transactional model from Sports, Media, and Society on a whiteboard and then spend much of the rest of the first real class period starting to mark it up (Wenner, 1989, p. 26). How do we locate athlete social media on this map? How do we conceptualize the new message flows enabled by social media? Do the original master categories still cohere? Where would we place an outlet like The Players'Tribune or a gambling company's content? In doing this I want to invite them to intervene in the systemic underpinnings of sports media right away. As such we begin to understand that media content must originate in one place and then travel to others.

The course meetings continue to focus on the professional identity and practice of the various job categories, with exercises in class discussion to bring these ideas down to everyday work. A discussion of the relationship between sports institutions and their media partners is often accompanied by an imagined University-of-Wisconsin-wide sports network to be marketed around the state. Our discussion of journalistic professionalism pairs with discussions of some of the barriers to women and people of color in sports media or the ways sports journalism often avoids concepts like violence against women and activism. Our discussion of agenda-setting in sports journalism often nicely pairs the latest research in the longitudinal studies on coverage of women's athletics (for example, Cooky et al., 2021). We can go further and do an appraisal of our local newspaper to lay out what the local news agenda looks like. We often just pull up the sports vertical of Milwaukee Journal-Sentinel here and count what sports get covered. Our discussion of sports sponsorship as a communicative practice is an entry point into how gambling messages find their way into game broadcasts and team-branded communication. In looking at practices, we can see how the social trends that manifest in sports appear and make sense of them in a discussion-based format. This section concludes with an introduction to social media, exploring the ways teams and athletes engage, and beginning to speak about fan cultures. Readings for these sections are a mix of practical (demystifying what it is people in these jobs do) and critical (looking broadly at what the potential effects of these defensible choices might be).

My approach has been to adapt the hands-on education techniques we use in our more openly practical classes for theory. The purpose of connecting sports and society is not to critique for its own sake. I want my students to see the ways ideas from sports sociology predict or explain the presence of specific types of content, and I want to build in opportunities to apply those ideas directly. The purpose of a class like this, after all, is to explore where the ideas do not apply. In both cases, I make heavy use of examples from contemporary sports media and build in-class assignments around that.

The downside of this format is that it does not lend itself to a set-it-and-forget-it style class, where the materials we use are evergreen. It is not a new prep, but it does mean that class materials change each year. At the same time, this lends itself to a specific assignment that I use in the discussion-based format, which asks students to bring in examples of the current week's theme, allowing them to lead to discussion. When student discussion leaders take this seriously, it often leads to the most productive classroom exchanges because they bring in the examples that are fully relevant to them. I believe that showing concrete examples speaks better to our professionally oriented students rather than speaking to broad cultural norms and the spread of ideas. As I get older, I fear the frame of reference I have around sports is less common than the one the students bring.

Teaching the Intersection of Sports and Society

The focus on media systems and professions in the first half of the course lays the groundwork for the idea that our experience with sports is thoroughly mediated. Every element of our experience with sports is produced in some way, framed for us. Even new actors like those on social media can contribute to our understanding of this space. The question we as scholars often ask is to what effect is all this effort put? Are the messages we receive through sports media transmissible into other contexts? For students who walked into the class resistant to that idea—sports are the break from "real life"—my goal is get them to consider the idea.

Early in this section of the course, I try to give my students a non-scholarly text to lay out this connection. I have tried a few, but the one I have had most success with is the legendary Leonard Koppett's chapter on "sport think" (Koppett, 1981) from his book **Sports Illusion, Sports Reality**. He argues that the habits of mind and language we develop around sports prime us to think that political life is about zero-sum outcomes and war is like a game. This is an old chapter, but in some ways the distance is helpful for students. The argument for the power of our mediated sports experience to shape the ways we engage with the broader world is basically an argument about hegemony. I have never found my undergraduate sports media students particularly receptive to those ideas in the abstract. The challenge of hegemony, of course, is that it is hard to see. The argument that Black athletes and White athletes receive differential treatment in media coverage is much easier for them to assimilate.

Again, my emphasis is on concrete examples and case studies. We are only a few years removed from the building of a new sports arena in Milwaukee, which means the literature on the ways teams push for new stadia feels relevant. In this instance, they can see the construction of local identity through the language around the teams and venue. We also can speak about the ways politicians attach themselves to sports to help build their own identities. The larger discussions remain highly relevant to them. The connections between UFC and the Trump campaign in 2024 or the appearance of Steve Kerr at the Democratic convention show the ways political actors and sporting figures interact to help extend their messages. As such, the sporting discourse can never be fully separable from a society's politics.

Throughout this part of the course, as I make these connections, I also encourage the students to build their own critiques. Often, they are uncomfortable with my analytic approach, which treats everything as a work in progress. I will lean into this idea at times if only to try to elicit a reaction. When students build their own accounts of how sports, media, and society fit together, I am eager to depart from my script to work through the implications of their ideas. I am also open about what I do and do not know. My invitations for them to fight me on concepts often go unheeded. But the connections they draw do make for a more interesting class period. My goal is to push them to think more deeply about how the fun-and-games, they want to connect to, affect the broader society. But I also do not have a distinct agenda beyond that. I do not hate sports, and I do not care if they start to hate sports. I do want them to understand sports and how they fit into society. Critique is more than just finding fault. It is about deep engagement.

I will conclude this discussion on teaching critique in sports with a critique of our own institutions. American institutions of higher education, and especially public universities, have articulated their value as vocational training for the incoming workforce. As I write this, my own university system has adopted a "War for Talent" framing to convince a skeptical state legislature to give us the funding the governor asked for in his budget. I understand that my bosses see appealing to the concept of value-for-money as more broadly palatable than talking about specific programs or, heaven forbid, the importance of the liberal arts. I am deeply uncomfortable with centering only market needs in justifying the value of education. While I very much welcome the growth of sports media programs at American universities, I also acknowledge that part of the institutional rationale reflects both the need to drive enrollment and the emphasis on job training in one of the American industries that appears to still be growing. McChesney (1989) once argued the broadly understood apolitical nature of sport made it a fixture in American media. It is not bad to train people for these jobs and help them find the connections to launch their careers. Teaching skills is one of the most important jobs professors have. But it is not the only thing we should be doing in higher education contexts. We have a responsibility to make sure that the next generation of sports professionals are at least familiar with ideas about the ways sports and sports media affect society.

References

Cooky, C., Council, L. T. D., Mears, M. A., & Messner, M. A. (2021). One and Done: The Long Eclipse of Women's Televised Sports, 1989–2019. *Communication and Sport*, *9*(3), 347–371. https://doi.org/10.1177/21674795211003524

Koppett, L. (1981). *Sports illusion, sports reality*. Houghton Mifflin.

McChesney, R. (1989). Media made sport: A history of sports coverage in the United States. In L. A. Wenner (Ed.), *Media, Sport, and Society* (pp. 49–70). Sage.

Wenner, L. A. (1989). The research agenda. In L. A. Wenner (Ed.), *Media, Sports & Society* (pp. 13–48). Sage.

Part V
Bonus: Practical Classroom Tips

14 **The Gym Bag**
Tips for Assignments and Class Activities
Welch Suggs, University of Georgia, and Lauren Reichart Smith, Rowan University

As you're planning your course, you should plan on avoiding two things: lecturing and war stories. By now, students tune out lectures, or at least retain just enough information to pass whatever test you may give them. It is not an effective way to convey information unless a) you are presenting theory or research results and b) you're really good at making that compelling. And while you may have a rich background of professional achievements and experiences, students will tune out stories about the old days if you use them too often.

Instead, most scholars of pedagogy will tell you to use active learning to the greatest extent possible. While this sounds like just another buzzword to come down from an academic-planning office, it encompasses a wide range of strategies to engage students and to get them to take ownership of their own learning. Rather than defining "active learning" and making an exhaustive list of strategies, we present a series of assignments and class activities you may find helpful in motivating students to lean forward and become involved in class, rather than sitting back and surreptitiously checking TikTok. Consider these things you can pack up and take to your class in a metaphorical gym bag.

Semester Starting Points

This Class Is Not Trivia Night

Kevin Hull, University of South Carolina

Sometimes classes that contain both the words "intro" and "sports" in them will attract students who think "this will be an easy A." They assume the hours they have spent watching ESPN over the years will mean they do not need to do any reading, pay attention to lectures, or do any additional work. In my experience, those students tend to do significantly worse than those who walk in with barely any sports knowledge on day one.

In hopes of weeding out and/or warning those students, I have learned that putting a very explicit statement in my syllabus and further reinforcing this fact on the first day is a good way to let them know what the class is. For my Sports, Media, and Society class, the introductory class in the Sports Media major, the statement below is directly from my syllabus under the heading "A PSA About This Course:"

If you are a diehard sports fan, that knowledge guarantees you nothing here. This is not a class about athletes, teams, statistics, and standings. This is a class about the sports media and the role that sporting events and athletes play in our society. This is not a class about sports trivia. If you know who won the 1997 American League Rookie of Year or can list each Super Bowl winner in reverse alphabetical order, that won't help you here. Several students in the past have assumed they didn't need to study, show up, or do the work because they were Joe/Jane SuperFan and those students have not done well. Don't fall into that trap.

While not a perfect solution, it at least warns students that they must work to be successful. Students in an introductory hands-on sports class could also benefit from a similar statement, but perhaps tailored to those classes. For example, a sports broadcasting syllabus might remind students that they will need to do research, interviews, and attend practices—not just show up to class and restate or opine about what happened in the big game the night before.

Introductory Survey and Prompts

Karen Turner and Claire Smith, Temple University

With The Influence of Sports Media on Modern Society class size limited to 19 students, it is easy to design ways for students to introduce themselves to each other and to the professor. One of the most innovative approaches introduced by Karen Turner was the "Introductory Assignment," where students complete a brief survey. As the students are advised:

This is a two-purpose assignment. First, it's an opportunity for us to get to know you. Second, we want to encourage you—if you haven't already—to actively think about how societal issues intersect with sports and how sports media cover these intersections. This assignment will help us assess how well you write, your media reading, listening, and viewing habits, plus your career goals.

We professors seek to understand their media currency, asking each student to explain what sources and resources they rely upon, specifically social media platforms, radio, television, blogs, influencers, newspapers, magazines, online sites, favorite sports apps, word-of-mouth, podcasts.

Because most of the students are juniors or seniors, many may already have media experience. They are therefore encouraged to share insights from their internships and/or work with student and professional media outlets.

It is also important for the professors to understand the "why" students have chosen the course. So, the deep dive asks about tools, pursuits, their observations and critiques of the profession and more. Included questions:

- *Will or are you pursuing the Klein Sports Media certificate?*
- *What outlets do you pay to use, either print or streaming?*
- *What are your course expectations, namely, what do you hope to get out of this course?*
- *What are the three most important course-related sports stories that unfolded in the semester prior to the one you are currently enrolled in? Why is each important? How well (or not) did the sports media cover the issues?*
- *Are there any specific course-related sports issues you want/expect to cover in the class?*

Then we ask the students to help guide the class going forward by naming the top three, in order of importance to them. Also, we seek to determine if there is a sport that they'd like to study in more depth to discover its impact on our society.

What these introductions often do is help guide a course that often rides the waves of current events. Over the years we have added topics such as sports betting, ageism and allyship. The students' interests help gauge if we, as professors, are meeting our own stated objectives of demonstrating how sports followers and influencers in the media also play a role in influencing modern society.

Use Student-Made Videos to Break the Ice

Welch Suggs, University of Georgia

In a mid-sized or smaller class (fewer than 40 students, in my experience), one of the best ways to get students to know you're paying attention to them is to learn their names and a little bit about how they carry themselves in the world as quickly as possible. Doing so not only builds a bond with them, but it also can give you an idea of what their big-picture goals and interests are, which in turn helps you give them feedback they'll find valuable and useful.

Instead of using icebreaker exercises or table tents for the first day or week of class, for the past few years I have been requiring students to produce short selfie videos introducing themselves to me and to their classmates. These are due before the first day of class, and I publish them so that the entire class can watch. Given the amount of time most students spend consuming handheld video, they are usually comfortable with this kind of content, and the TikTokers among them can be very creative. I do one of my own afresh for each semester to humanize myself and usually do something to mix it up, such as recording while walking my dog or riding my mountain bike.

Here is the prompt from my Introduction to Reporting and Writing for Sports course:

Produce a 60–90 second video introducing yourself to your instructors and the class. Have fun with it and be creative, but please include the following points:

- *Your name and what you prefer to be called, especially if it's different from what shows up in* [our learning management system]. *Please mention accent marks or other things so we can all get it right.*

- *Which pronouns you use* (I link to UGA's College of Education's guidelines on this)
- *Your year in college and your major*
- *Your hometown and high school*
- *A little about your background in sports*
- *What your dream job would be*
- *What skills you're most interested in learning or polishing.*

Here are some suggestions for producing:

- *Write out what you want to say beforehand, but don't just read a script. You want to feel natural.*
- *Act like you're talking to someone; don't just stare at the screen and talk.*
- *Control your background, including both the video background and the audio you can hear. Try to avoid having a ceiling fan in the background.*
- *There are teleprompter apps you can use (both for this assignment and standup videos you'll be producing later in class), but frankly they're more trouble than they're worth.*
- Finally, I include a selfie video of my own.

Foundational Assignments

Game Journal

Kacey Doran, Rowan University

What's a shorter project that's useful as a check-in a couple times a semester and more fun than a paper or a quiz for the student to create and the professor to grade? My suggestion is to have your students do a Game Journal.

- Assignment and goals: Use a short video format to give your students a chance to do a low-stakes project, practice digital editing and focusing on one concept. This helps to avoid students summarizing without effectively showing you that they fully understand an important term, the significance of an important moment in history, and the like.

- For esports students, have them film and share five minutes on how a concept from class applies to their favorite video game or esports, depending on whether it relates to the competitive scene or more broadly to game design.
- Use a secure streaming platform with a sharable link or an accessible online school platform.
- For sports students, they can use a traditional sports video game like those in the Madden or NBA 2k series, or they can talk over a video of live sports footage if you're able to get them legal access for academic use. Again, have them take five minutes to show how a concept from class applies to a moment in the game, crowd reactions, and so forth.

Using Fantasy Sports as a Teaching Tool

Lauren Reichart Smith, Rowan University

When considering what sports communication and media students are often very passionate about and will easily engage with, gambling is one that immediately comes to mind. However, because I'm guessing none of our universities would be thrilled with us running a class gambling ring, fantasy sports becomes a much better alternative. I started using fantasy sports as a teaching tool several years ago, and have adapted it to fit the needs of a couple of different courses (Managing Sports Media, and Organizational Communication in Sports).

The broad idea is simple—break students into groups, who will then 'manage' a team's media and communication over the course of the semester, with the assignments geared toward topics and concepts that the course covers. Students seem much more engaged with this type of project than using a theoretical situation or organization to apply what they are learning. Based on the needs of your course, different assignments can be substituted in or adapted. I currently work with this basic framework:

- All About the Team: The groups will each select a city that their team will be based in, come up with a team name and mascot, and provide information about their fan base—primarily demographics (usually it's easier if the city they select already has a team—I allow them to use the demographic information from the real team).

- Draft Day: Pick one class day and hold the fantasy draft live in class. It's usually fun for the students, especially when one group drafts a player other groups were wanting.

- Media Plan/Strategy: Here students need to look at the media market of their city to determine what media outlets are there, consider what owned media their team possesses, and build a media strategy.

- Speech policy: Have them come up with a policy on what players are/are not allowed to say on social media or in interviews (for example, hate speech will not be tolerated).

- Create stories: I usually have students create five stories about their team over the course of the semester. Story topics can vary from a game recap, team feature, player feature, responding to a situation with a player (if one goes out with an injury, for example), or community outreach events. I adapt these based on the specific needs of each course.

- Crisis plan: Here students create a plan for how the team will handle a crisis should it occur.

- Crisis day: One day during the semester, with no warning, I come into the class and announce that it is crisis day. I give all the teams a crisis, and using their crisis plan, strategies of apologia, and potentially their speech policy, have them craft a response to the crisis. I have used PED use, illegal gambling, illegal drug use, harassment, DUI's, violence, or inappropriate behavior as bases for the crises I create.

Finally, I do award a couple of extra credit points to the league champion. That way, the students will actually play their team, rather than create it and forget it.

Brand Partnership Pitch Development

Cara Hawkins-Jedlicka, Washington State University

Instead of lecturing about sponsorship strategies or assigning theoretical case study analyses, I have been running an in-class activity where students develop and present actual brand partnership proposals using real athletes and companies. This exercise not only teaches practical skills but also helps students understand how values alignment, audience demographics, and local market dynamics influence successful partnerships in today's business landscape.

Pre-Class Preparation for the Instructor

- Review provided pitch template and evaluation criteria (see below)
- Research potential local/regional brand partners
- Identify collegiate athletes whose values and audience align with the chosen brand
- Prepare preliminary market research on target demographics

In-Class Small Group Work (Teams of 3–4)

- Select one collegiate athlete (I often have them draw an athlete from a hat)
- Choose one brand partner from the approved list or propose an alternative
- Complete a pitch template following this structure:
  - Greeting: Keep it simple, for example, Hi [brand].
  - Introduction: Include athlete's name, sport, school, and any defining characteristics that set them apart from other influencers. Establish credibility quickly.
  - Connection to the brand: Share what the athlete likes about the brand to illustrate why brand and athlete want to work together. Add a personalized detail, such as favorite product or how long they've been using the brand.
  - Request: Share partnership idea or ask for more information. For example, "I would love to share a TikTok series showcasing your brand with my community. Could you please share the best contact for discussing a potential partnership?"
  - Closing: End with goodwill. For example, best regards, have a great day, thank you, and so forth.
- Develop a five-minute presentation with visual aids.

Presentation and Feedback Session

- Each group presents their pitch to the class
- Explain strategic reasoning behind athlete-brand pairing
- Field questions from classmates acting as "brand executives"

- The instructor provides industry perspective on realistic market potential.

Learning Objectives

- Analyze values alignment between personal brands and corporate sponsors
- Practice professional presentation and persuasion skills
- Apply market research to strategic decision-making.

The Blog

Brian Moritz, St. Bonaventure University

This assignment combines two important skills for sports journalism students—covering a beat and keeping a blog. The length of time can be adjusted based on the length of a course. This three-week blog assignment is a part of a seven-week asynchronous online course, but it can go longer. Here's what I provide students:

Starting Instructions

This is a multi-week assignment that combines blogging and beat writing.

For the next three weeks, you will be a beat writer for a team, conference, league or sport of your choice. You'll cover that beat for a blog that you create on your own website.

You get to choose your beat. You have complete freedom in this. But as Uncle Ben told us years ago, with great freedom comes great responsibility. (Wait … that's not, that's not what he … you know, let's just move on.) You should pick a beat that:

- You care deeply about: I don't mean you have to be a big fan of the team (there are reasons why you shouldn't do that). But you do have to care enough to follow and keep up with the beat enough to be an expert on it.
- You have access to: If you are able to interview people on your beat, be there in person for games and events, it will make for a much better blog than just another Pittsburgh Penguins blog (or whatever).

Assignment Requirements

Create a separate page on your existing Wordpress site for your blog.

You must create a minimum of three posts a week, no more than one per day. (This is so you don't post three times on Sunday night and call it a week). You can do more than three. You can do as many as you like. However, you cannot do less.

All posts must be at least 100 words long.

At least one of your weekly posts must be a reported piece, where you do original (not aggregated) reporting.

You are responsible for any and all news that happens on your beat. If there is big national news involving your team conference or team, you'll be expected to cover it and write about it.

If there's no "news" on your beat that week? Welp, you still have to do at least three posts. So, get creative.

The Way in which the Assignment Breaks Down

- Week 4 (5% of assignment grade): A minimum of three posts about your beat, with one post including original reporting.
- Week 5 (5% of assignment grade): A minimum of three posts about your beat, with one post including original reporting.
- Week 6 (5% of assignment grade): A minimum of three posts about your beat.
- One of the three posts MUST be a column (A 500-word opinion piece).

The Deadline Gamer

Welch Suggs, University of Georgia

Thanks to changes in the news business, the true deadline gamer—a story filed the moment the game ends—is all but dead. People can find all the information they need from box scores or the ESPN ticker, or they may choose to wait for the hot takes from studio shows. But it's still valuable for students to learn how to watch a game, process the information, and be able to communicate clearly why one team won, the key moments and statistics that explain why that team won, and what the victory (or loss) means in the overall context of a season.

I typically work out an arrangement with a professional or collegiate team to host a specified number of students to cover a game and sit in on media availabilities afterwards. Students feel the excitement and the intensity of being in a professional atmosphere, and the opportunity to interview players and coaches is something they take very seriously. And the deadline pressure raises both the nerves and the excitement of seeing it through. This is the culminating assignment in the foundational sports media class, and even though it is the first class they take, many graduating students remember it as one of their favorite moments in our program.

Students practice components of the assignment for earlier game-coverage assessments in the term as well as for homework.

This particular assignment consists of four parts:

- Prep:
  - *Team records, overall and conference*
  - *Team last five results*
  - *Players: team leaders, league/national leaders*
  - *How teams and players were doing last year at this point in the season*
  - *Notes on transfers and newcomers*
  - *Key moments/results/developments this season*
- I also have them write final sentences with team records and next games beforehand.
- Buzzer: *Due at the buzzer: your choice of…*
  - *Bullet-point takeaways, written as complete sentences with a 2–3 sentence lede paragraph*
    - *Keys to the game (at least five)*
    - *What we learned (at least five)*
  - *AP-style recap: A 250-word summary of the game, noting key stats and moments as with the first gamer.*
- Write-thru/video recap: *Due approximately 90 minutes postgame, your choice of…*
  - *A 400-word write-thru game story incorporating quotes*
  - *A 75–90-second video recap, incorporating at least one piece of A-roll from interviews*

- Due 24 hours after the game in a group of three or four: *15-minute podcast explaining why the game turned out the way it did and what we learned from teams.*

Each phase of the assignment is weighted equally. In addition to executing on deadline, students learn to focus not on their opinions about the game and the teams involved, but how to tell stories straight and to get their information correct. And providing options gives students a chance to practice the skills they want to use in the future, podcasting being a hot one right now among mine. We also emphasize the importance of deadlines and accuracy: A factual error results in a 50% deduction in points for that phase, and missing deadline results in a 0. I evaluate each phase based on grammar and usage, style, structure and coherency, and whether students correctly identify critical elements. At the end of it, they are usually exhausted but exhilarated. It makes for fun conversations being among the last people walking out of the venue.

The Lifecycle of a Media Credential

Betsy Emmons, University of Nebraska

Media credentials, as discussed in the public-relations chapter, allow access to various areas of sporting events to allow media members to complete their work. With social media influencing and non-traditional media outlets offering content to viewers as likely as television networks, having a system in place for media credential approval is important when working sporting events.

Credential requests for mega-events like the Super Bowl or the Olympics number in the thousands. How do public relations and communications staff decide who gets one and who does not? Since it is important to allow media access to areas of an event that need to be crowd-controlled, such as locker rooms and sidelines, allowing everyone access to such areas becomes problematic and even dangerous.

With a partner, brainstorm a list of requirements for a media credential for a popular sporting event. Reflect on the balance between wanting to allow coverage of the event but also prioritizing access for some media over others. Some variables to consider:

- What video network will be televising the event? What sort of access should competing networks get and why?

- What about global interest? Think about the importance of global interest in the event and if there is a healthy balance among media to reach diverse audiences.
- What sort of policy should there be for social media influencers? Should influencers have access at all? If so, what rules will be in place for determining who gets a credential and who does not?
- Which websites/digital media groups should get credentials and why?
- Consider local media. What city media should get access? Remember the importance of maintaining a strong relationship of support with the local community.

Something About Swag

Nicole Kraft, Ohio State University

During the semester, we explore ethical scenarios where students apply ethical values or legal precedent to real-world, contemporary scenarios. The goal of these exercises is to help bring ethics to life for them. This is what I provide for students:

Objectives

- Apply what we have learned related to ethics to a real-life scenario.
- Defend your ethical decision-making using ethical theory and the AP Sports Editors Code.

The Scenario

You are covering Ohio State football all season, and they make the College Football National Championship game. The game takes place in the Rose Bowl, and you fly out, funded by The Lantern. While there you stay in the media hotel where they provide a full prime-rib and lobster buffet with open bar every night, along with a package of swag that includes a Rose Bowl National Championship backpack, polo shirt and engraved AirPods.

Ohio State ends up winning the game and becomes the National Champion! A month after the game they provide framed posters of the game-winning play with a plate on the frame that states, "Thank you for your coverage of the National Championship Ohio State Buckeyes."

You must decide:

- Is it ethical to eat at the buffet and drink at the open bar? Why?
- Is it ethical to accept the media swag provided by the Rose Bowl/CFB playoff? Why?
- Is it ethical to accept the Ohio State post-season gift? Why?
- Discuss in your table team and decide which, if any of these, are acceptable options.
- The team lead will write up your decision and validate it in 100–200 words.
- Create a policy for your newsroom personnel to follow now and in the future.
- Have team lead submit to the learning management system.

Group Projects

Group Charters

Candy Lee, Northwestern University

If you have groups working together on projects, you might ask them to consider a "charter" before they dive into the project itself. As they work on roles and responsibilities, they begin to assess each other's strengths, and decide on when to ignore some irritations (a member lags in work or does not show up for meetings).

Questions for the charter

- How will meetings be set?
- What roles do we need and who will undertake them?
- What resources and processes are required?
- Who has authority to make decisions?
- What to do when a person is not pulling their weight?

- What about someone who shows up but does not speak out?
- How will we know when we have achieved agreement?
- What do we do if we feel we are doing more work than others?
- What kind of personality types do we have on this team?
- There will be disagreements so what do we do then?
- What does success look like?

Collaborative Ground Rules Creation

Cara Hawkins-Jedlicka, Washington State University

In any course where discussion and peer interaction are central, one of the biggest challenges is creating an environment where all students feel safe to share, question, and even disagree respectfully. Traditional approaches often involve the instructor imposing discussion rules from the top down, but this misses an opportunity for students to invest in the community they're helping to create. I make students collaboratively create their own ground rules. This gives them ownership over their learning environment while ensuring the norms reflect what they actually need to engage.

Collaborative Ground Rules Creation Process

Step 1:

- Students access shared digital bulletin board (Padlet or similar platform)
- Each student submits 1–2 potential ground rules for class discussions
- Prompts: "What do you need to feel safe sharing ideas?" "What behaviors help you learn best in group settings?"
- Submissions are anonymous to encourage honesty.

Step 2:

- All submitted rules are displayed for class viewing
- Students vote on their top 5–7 favorites
- Brief small-group discussions about why certain rules resonated
- Final set of ground rules is established by consensus

Ongoing Implementation:

- Ground rules are posted prominently in classroom and online
- Mid-semester check-in: "How are we doing with our agreements?"
- Students can propose modifications or additions as needed
- Gentle reminders to reference "our agreements" rather than "my rules."

Sample Student-Generated Ground Rules:

- "We listen and we don't judge"
- "It's okay to change your mind"
- "Acknowledge when you don't know something"
- "Wait for another person to respond or three minutes before sharing again."

Let All Students Grade Group Presentations

Chris Roberts, University of Alabama

Group projects can be a pain because you must grade them, and because students may bicker among themselves and/or complain to you about group members who bully or don't do their share of the work.

A solution: Let students help you grade. Immediately after a presentation ends, have students in the audience rate the presentation, while individual members in the presenting group rate themselves and everyone in the group using a rubric I provide early in the semester.

The survey language is adopted from others to build two online survey instruments. I suggest Cornell's Center for Teaching Innovation (n.d.) for its useful "How to evaluate group work" page.

1   Students in the audience take a survey with a 1–5 scale for quality of topic, quality of presentation, "kept my attention," and "application of what we learned in class." Each student also writes a general note about the presentation. They are promised confidentiality.

2   Students who just presented use a different survey, where they rate each group member and themselves on a variety of topics. They confidentially use a scale to rate themselves and every other group

member on the level of contribution, the attitude, punctuality and meeting deadlines, communication among members, and quality of work. There's a space to leave a comment about any or all members, or a general comment. Finally, I pose the question: "If you had a dollar to divide among yourself and members, how many pennies would each of you receive?" It's not perfect, but the confidentiality provides an insight into group dynamics.

I make my own notes during each presentation, but later calculate median scores for each part of the survey for each group. Each group receives the data, my notes, and also the (anonymous) peer comments that prove useful. The in-group surveys allow each student to grade individual students for in-group dynamics.

Center for Teaching Innovation. (n.d.). *How to evaluate group work*. Cornell University. https://teaching.cornell.edu/teaching-resources/active-collaborative-learning/collaborative-learning/how-evaluate-group-work

Topical Discussions

How to Not be a "Homer"

Chris Roberts, University of Alabama

ESPN's Rece Davis earned his degree from the University of Alabama, but you wouldn't know it by listening to him. The *College Gameday* host plays it straight on and off air, and he calls himself "on scholarship to ESPN" when people ask about allegiances. Davis is not a "homer"—a sports journalist (or anyone) whose judgment is clouded by being a fan or a particular team, player, or coach. He is respected—high praise among fans.

How can you learn to not be a "homer?" We suggest:

- Practice: Assign students to attend or watch a game of their favorite team and never stand or cheer.
- Learning to recognize it's a "good play" even when the other team made the good play.
- Let the replay, not your heart or wishes, decide whether an official's call was correct.

- Not betting on games.

- Not wearing the color of either team when covering a game.

- Being consistent with interviewing coaches and players. Saying "good luck" before a game and "congratulations" to a winner is fine. Screaming, high-fiving or crying is not. And don't ask for autographs for yourself.

- Watching true professionals at work.

Listen to an Interviewer's Questions, not the Answers

Chris Roberts, The University of Alabama

ESPN's Paul Finebaum doesn't have made-for-TV good looks, didn't play sports, majored in political science, and sometimes seems bored when taking random calls on his talk show. What makes him watchable is what a fellow ESPN broadcaster said about him in 2018: "If you asked me who are the two greatest interviewers on radio and television, I would say Paul Finebaum and Howard Stern."

Finebaum consistently draws interesting information and ideas from his guests. It's likely because he started as a print news reporter, where he gained attention by asking good questions and breaking stories that did not always flatter the subject.

Only later did Finebaum move into opinion columns and then into radio, where his reporting skills and asking questions give him with the facts he uses when offering opinions.

The next time you watch Finebaum or other sports journalist interview someone, don't immediately listen for the answers. (You could record and show an interview with a newsmaker and discuss it in class.) Have students listen to questions when an interview has a coach, athletic director, athlete, or other newsmaker. Note how the best interviews have short questions so the guest does most of the talking. The interviewer doesn't interrupt. And the interviewer listens to answers, leading to better follow-up questions.

Index

inspiration porn 35–6
intentionality 23, 25

James, LeBron 65, 148
Janovy, Jena 129
Jim Crow 149
John Huland Carmical Sports Media
    Institute 131
Johnson, Earvin "Magic," 116
Johnson, Mark E. 131–3
Jordan, Michael 149

Kaepernick, Colin 148
Kerr, Steve 156
Klein College of Media and
    Communication 139–40
Koppett, Leonard 155

League of Legends 100
LGBTQ+ 147, 149
Life as Matt 147
Los Angeles Kings 122

Major League Baseball (MLB) 75,
    123, 139, 140, 143
Manley, Effa 144
Mason Dixon Line 144
MassLive 127
MaxPreps 107
Mays, Willie 144
media center 54–5, 58
media credential
    and ethics 9, 13–14
    and granting credentials to
        54–5, 172–3
    and requesting 108–10
media relations 15, 53–4, 105, 108,
    111, 133–4

media theory 4, 86
media training 53, 60
Michaelis, Vicki 131–3
Milwaukee Journal-Sentinel 154
Missouri Method 105
Model of Athlete Brand Image
    (MABI) 81

Name, Image and Likeness (NIL)
    3, 14, 59–60, 79–81, 84,
    86, 108
National Association for
    Intercollegiate Athletics
    (NAIA) 108
National Basketball Association
    (NBA) 66, 75, 116, 145,
    148, 166
National Collegiate Athletic
    Association (NCAA)
    divisions and conferences 107–8
    and gambling 18
    and Name, Image and Likeness
        (NIL) 80–1
National Football League (NFL)
    75, 123
National Hockey League (NHL) 122
National Junior College Athletic
    Association (NJCAA) 108
Negandhi, Kevin 140
Negro Leagues 144–5
New Jersey Devils 122
New York Daily News 118
New York Times 140
news organizations 106, 127,
    129, 134

Ohio State University, The 3, 133–4
Olympics 31, 38, 131–2, 172

About the Editors

Welch Suggs (ORCID: 0000-0002-0133-9191) is associate director of the Carmical Sports Media Institute at the University of Georgia and an associate professor of journalism. He has served in both roles since 2012. Dr. Suggs and colleagues developed an undergraduate certificate curriculum in sports media for Georgia's College of Journalism and Mass Communication, with alumni now working for a range of media organizations including ESPN, the *Washington Post*, the PGA Tour, and numerous NFL, NBA, MLB and MLS teams. Suggs' research includes work in both sports media and college athletics policy, and he is a past officer and head of AEJMC's Sports Communication Interest Group. He is the author of *A Place on the Team: The Triumph and Tragedy of Title IX* and numerous peer-reviewed journal articles and chapters. He was a journalist for ten years prior to re-entering academia, having served on the launch team of *Street & Smith's Sports Business Journal* and as senior editor for athletics at *The Chronicle of Higher Education*.

Lauren Reichert Smith (ORCID: 0000-0001-7017-5525) is a professor and the director for research initiatives for the Center for Sports Communication and Social Impact at Rowan University. Dr. Smith's main research area lies in media sport—the intersection between sports and mass media. Her research focuses on the effects of sports media on our emotions. She is the co-editor of *Communication and Contradiction in the NCAA: An Unlevel Playing Field* and numerous peer-reviewed journal articles and book chapters. Her work with the Center at Rowan focuses on the social impact of sports on local communities and industry partners. She is currently the Executive Director for the International Association of Communication and Sport.

About the Contributors

Kacey Doran is the Academic Esports Program Coordinator for the Sports Communication & Media Program as well as the Journalism Department at Rowan University. She has her doctorate in Childhood Studies from Rutgers University-Camden and her research centers gender, identity, and culture in esports and videogames. Her previous degrees include an M.A. in Children's Literature and a B.A. in Women's and Gender Studies, and her previous work experience includes teaching for competitive music programs, summer art programs, and library stacks management.

Betsy Emmons (ORCID: 0000-0002-3761-2065) is an associate professor of sports promotion in the College of Journalism and Mass Communications at the University of Nebraska-Lincoln. Dr. Emmons previously taught at Samford University in Birmingham, Alabama, where she also helped develop the sports media minor program and taught the public relations course sequence. She is active in the Public Relations Society of America and the Association for Education in Journalism and Mass Communications (AEJMC) sports communication interest group, serving as chair in 2023–2024. She is also a member of AEJMC's public relations division. Before her academic career, she was a public relations professional in the sports, travel, non-profit and consulting industries.

Steve Fox is a senior lecturer in journalism at the University of Massachusetts Amherst. He has 25 years of experience as an editor and reporter for print and online publications, including ten years as an editor in various capacities at *The Washington Post's* award-winning Web site. Before joining *The Post*, he was a sportswriter and editor at different publications for about 10 years, including serving as the national college basketball writer for United Press International. Steve has been involved with Web journalism since the mid-1990s. He joined *The Washington Post's* Web site in 1996, just months after the site went live on the Web. He edited one of the first news blogs on the Web and planned and edited multiple multimedia projects at *The Post*.

Cara Hawkins-Jedlicka (ORCID: 0000-0003-0163-3953) is an assistant professor of practice at Washington State University. She has more than a decade's worth of experience as a content producer and strategic communicator specializing in digital advertising strategy, with an emphasis on social media and online communities. Her research examines the intersection of brand, women's sport communication and influencer culture. Notably, her recent publications shed light on the evolving brand images of women athletes, particularly in the context of the Name, Image, and Likeness. She is the co-founder of the oral history podcast, Starting Line 1928, which documents the lived experiences of women distance running pioneers.

Nick Hirshon (ORCID: 0000-0002-5905-5677) is an associate professor at William Paterson University in New Jersey. Dr. Hirshon has written extensively about the history of sports media, including his book *We Want Fish Sticks: The Bizarre and Infamous Rebranding of the New York Islanders* as well as academic journal articles on baseball and bowling. Hirshon was a reporter from 2005 to 2011 for the *New York Daily News*.

Kevin Hull (ORCID: 0000-0001-6461-4069) is the sports media lead and an associate professor at the School of Journalism and Mass Communications at the University of South Carolina. As a former television sports broadcaster, his research focuses on how sportscasters at local television stations are adapting to a changing media environment. Dr. Hull is the author of two textbooks published by Human Kinetics: *Sports Broadcasting* and *Sports, Media, and Society*.

Nicole Kraft (ORCID: 0000-0002-9721-3664) is an associate professor of journalism practice at The Ohio State University, where she teaches Sports Journalism, Media Writing and Editing, Sports Media Relations, Feature Writing and Media Law and Ethics. Dr. Kraft is director of Ohio State's Sports & Society Initiative and vice chair of the Ohio State Athletics Council. Nicole is author of the books *Always Get the Name of the Dog: A Guide to Media Interviewing*, *Writing Fabulous Features* and *100 Years in Harness*. She and Kathleen Culver edited *Teaching Media Ethics*, released in 2024. She is an award-winning sportswriter who covers the Columbus Blue Jackets for the Associated Press, sports media for Forbes.com, and horseracing and auto racing for the *Columbus Dispatch*.

Candy Lee (ORCID: 0009-0000-7728-9031) is a professor at Medill at Northwestern University in Chicago and Evanston, Illinois. Dr. Lee teaches in the faculties of journalism and integrated marketing communications. Lee's research looks at leadership in several contexts including voice, communication and technology. She had a long career in marketing and communications in the private sector. She is involved in organizations across the Northwestern campus including the board of the student newspaper, The Daily Northwestern. Lee serves as a faculty advisor at the Buffett Institute for Global Affairs and has taught at some of the global partner schools. Her work on cross-university committees included provost's undergraduate task force, committee on athletics, wellness task force, CTEC evaluation, academic residential spaces, library oversight, Faculty Senate, curriculum committees and search committees.

Tammy Ray Matthews (ORCID: 0000-0002-0295-1438) is an assistant professor in the online sports journalism and digital journalism programs at St. Bonaventure University. Dr. Matthews had nearly 20 years of experience in major-market media, including serving as special sections editor for the *Chicago Sun-Times* and its north suburban subsidiaries. Matthews' research expertise is in studying global sports experiences, Namibia specifically, as well as delving into queer theories, storytelling, language, feminist theories, oral histories, social media and journalism.

Michael Mirer (ORCID: 0000-0003-2546-914X) is an assistant professor of communication at the University of Wisconsin-Milwaukee. Dr. Mirer has taught sports, media, and society courses since 2017. His research deals primarily with professional identity in sports journalism (and beyond) and the ways new entries into the media system shape professional practices.

Brian Moritz (ORCID: 0000-0001-6961-6442) examines the societal, organizational and economic models of digital journalism, with a particular focus on sports journalism. Dr. Moritz is an associate professor and director of online journalism MA programs at St. Bonaventure University and previously taught at SUNY Oswego and Syracuse University. He co-authored a textbook on sports journalism, *Introduction to Sports Journalism*, published by Human Kinetics in 2024. He is also author of the Sports Media Guy newsletter. His research has been published in *Communication & Sport* and the *International Journal of Communication & Sport*, as well as in several collected anthologies, and he is a frequent presenter at national and international conferences.

Claire Smith is founding executive director of the Claire Smith Center for Sports Media at Temple University and an assistant professor of practice in the department of journalism. A pathbreaking sportswriter, she was the first woman to cover a major-league baseball beat full-time, covering the New York Yankees for the *Hartford Courant* for half a decade before becoming the second national baseball columnist in the country. In 1990, Smith moved on to *The New York Times*, where she became that paper's first national baseball columnist, holding that position for eight years. She moved on to the *Philadelphia Inquirer* in 1998, where she served as an assistant sports editor and columnist until 2007. She then took the position of coordinating editor at ESPN, working for the multimedia giant from 2007 to 2021. In 2016 she was named the 68th recipient of the Baseball Writers Association of America's Career Excellence Award, the highest honor a baseball writer can receive. She has received pioneer awards from The National Association of Black Journalists and The Association for Women in Sports Media.

Karen M. Turner recently retired after 31 years as a professor of journalism at Temple University. Turner's professional journey is marked by notable stints as a reporter at various radio stations including WCTC-AM in New Jersey, and WPEN-AM in Philadelphia. Her research interests, deeply impactful in the realms of new media technologies, race studies, journalism pedagogy, and media diversity, have made significant contributions to the academic community. She is a 2020–21 recipient of Temple University's most prestigious Great Teacher award. Turner has been a guiding force in directing programs like Klein GO London and leading international reporting programs in Johannesburg and Cape Town, South Africa. Beyond academia, Turner is a long-time avid sports enthusiast. Being in the first class of women at Dartmouth College, she and a friend bucked the norm at the time by becoming the first women managers of the freshmen men's basketball team. Turner is also an advocate for quality journalism and intelligent talk radio. Her compassion extends to her canine companions, reflecting her multifaceted personality and interests.